# I Was Born Twice

## STORIES OF SYRIA'S TEARS

HASAN ALMOSSA

Copyright © 2019 by Hasan Almossa

All rights reserved. No part of this book may be used or reproduced by any means, graphic, electronic, or mechanical, including photocopying, recording, taping, or by any information storage retrieval system, without the written permission of the publisher except in the case of brief quotations embodied in critical articles and reviews.

Translated by Sami Karaali
Editing by Marcia Lynx Qualey & Diana Khanafer

To all those who were born without homes, lived without names, and died without graves.

And to those who were born twice, died several times, but are still alive.

The pinnacle of pain is when you too complain to the dead about what the living have been doing.

# Table of Contents

Introduction................................................................1

My Notebook................................................................4

The Reborn................................................................7

No Time For Joy................................................................40

Perfumes in Memory................................................................66

When will my fingers grow?................................................................80

The Strange Grave................................................................89

Kidnapping................................................................105

Suns drowning in the mud................................................................121

World Without Names................................................................136

From the Days of Siege................................................................165

Unfinished Story................................................................220

Last Call for Peace................................................................222

# Introduction

This book is neither a novel nor an autobiography nor a work of history to document the Syrian Revolution, which was turned into a senseless war that has torn apart my homeland. Instead, it is a combination of all three. I lived through this war and its consequences twice: First, when it stole the best years of my youth, when I was in secondary school and had been full of joy and wild dreams. Second, when the stories of other war victims, to whom I have dedicated my life, unfolded before my eyes. I have experienced their deepest pains, living their tragedies as they were forced to re-taste them after raging waves of war washed them away from their previous lives and homes. These were lives they worked long years to build, and all of it was demolished in moments.

The searing flames of this war have searched for these victims and scorched their souls even in their exile, preventing them from sleeping and thwarting their peace of mind.

I have lived the details of this war, which exist in the deep wrinkles on the faces of the old and the withered dreams wilting inside the eyes of children, as well as the tragedies behind the tears of widows and grieving mothers.

Although this is not a personal story nor a scholarly history nor an invented tale, elements from all these literary arts can be found in the book.

The stories and narratives are as I have seen them, and they include incidents I witnessed and tales I heard while living amongst thousands of war-oppressed people who have been left out of the historical records.

*Introduction*

Storytelling has become the art of our time that can convey speeches, languages, styles, and views. Hence, it is both the art that conveys the beauty of literature, and the mirror that reflects the reality with all its nuances. It is a tool to convey the difficult struggle between the self and the subject.

Through the pages of this book, I am the narrator. Yet this is not a personal autobiography, even though it includes a lot of my personal life, its social and psychological developments, especially at the beginning. I did not aim to write about myself, but it was necessary to explain the sudden transformations through which I changed from a teen who dreamed about his future and his personal life, into a man who puts his self and dreams away in order to live the lives of those who have been displaced—those who were forced to live in the open before they even made it to a tent.

My daily personal life overlaps with the lives of those whose stories I tell.

This book is a piece of nonfiction. I have not changed the dates and places of the events, although I have changed the names of its real-life characters for mere reasons of safety.

Some might think this is a history book documenting a specific period of time in my homeland Syria. Indeed, this book might be considered informal history, as I tried to get through details that history books usually neglect. Their pages only focus on major events and names, ignoring the consequences of those events on ordinary humans and victims who have lived between the lines, completely overshadowed. Thus, I have aimed at documenting the pains suffered by those people who tend to be thrown into the dusty drawers of history.

*Introduction*

Finally, as this book has been written throughout a now seven-year-long war in my homeland Syria, you might wonder what the relation between its stories and the ongoing war might be. The war described in my book is the social reality and the main source of conflict that forms the base for my stories. These stories document a society during war with all its heart-wrenching war history.

As I tried to paint an image of the war and its impact on humans, I also tried to document and portray the killings and destructive tools of war: life in exile, solitude, forced displacement, bombings, kidnapping, detention, torture, family separation, sickness, mental illness, disability, and hopelessness. I wanted every story in the book to focus on one or more than one of these elements, but most stories unintentionally include all of them.

Every person in this book embodies a handful of other human beings within the depths of its story. Mariam can represent the thousands of women who died waiting to see their children again. Um Aziz reminds us of all the women whose hearts and homes have been crushed by war. Lilan represents all children who are waiting for their dead parents to come back. Osman is the thousands of detainees who have become soul-less numbers, longing for death to escape regular torture.

In short, the following pages are meant to immortalize the stories of these characters because they represent the forgotten majority of war victims about whom no one talks.

# My Notebook

**Dear reader,**

More than once, you will read the phrase, "I wrote in my notebook." So, what is this notebook?

Unlike humans, who usually bear only one name throughout their lifetimes, the notebook goes by many. However, there is a common thread between this notebook and humans. Both go through different phases.

In each phase, the notebook was gradually shaped, growing like a plant until I managed to transfer it into this book to not get lost, as had happened several times before.

But now, this notebook's spirit has been captured in the book, forging a telepathic link with my memory that tried to save everything, while only a little remained.

As narrow as a palm, and as small as a child, my notebook began its journey in life: I used to put it in my pocket to jot down people's questions and inquiries. I also wrote down names and addresses of patients and the injured, so I could follow up with them in the future.

So my notebook grew, as I wrote more and more. I wrote about war, common sayings and poems, and some stories. I wrote about pain as it was lived by ordinary people. Publishing was not a goal I had in mind during the writing process, for I rather wrote to remember people's pain, to follow up on their stories, and to solve their problems. Later, I started gathering the

*My Notebook*

sorts of details that most media outlets cannot focus on. These, these are the important details.

Even though I was recording such details so as never to lose them, my notebook was lost more than once, at many times irretrievable.

In 2015, I lost it for good, so I tried to collect the fragments of information remaining in my memory, as well as some things I had scribbled down on small sheets of paper. With every name I wrote, I tried to restore my notebook. But many questions would pop into my thoughts without answers.

What happened to the one who'd dreamed of going to Europe? Did he ever arrive, or was he trapped in a prison on his way? Did he disappear inside the belly of the ocean's big whale?

What happened to that woman who came with her injured son? Is he still alive, or has he died and left his mother wandering through a cruel life?

What happened to the old man who was asking for a prosthetic leg? Did he ever get it, or does he still live with a cane?

What about the girl whose father promised her a new eye while she was riding in the ambulance? Did she ever get a new eye, or was her father only trying to soothe her pain?

What about that family who sold all of their property to travel to Europe? Did the human trafficker keep his promise and help them to reach Germany?

The act of reorganizing the information in my notebook brought up thousands of questions and put me in front of hundreds of unforgettable stories. Many of these stories were too painful to document, and I was afraid,

*My Notebook*

too, that my bag would become as heavy as mountains. There are too many graves in exile: solitary graves, group graves, and lost graves. It was hard for me to put the destruction of the past, present, and future in my bag and sleep beside it every night.

I needed to sleep to continue my work, yet how could my eyes taste soothing rest alongside all these tragedies?

And so, I was sleepless as I relived these human tragedies day after day. I often wished a bullet had ended my life so that I did not have to re-witness these stories I was encumbered by.

The buzz of bullet stayed with me, for three months. It kept on visiting me from time to time. I wished to fall asleep eternally, or, as to avoid any euphemisms, experience a minor death, in order to comfort my tired soul. Others wished to relax forever and turn to the real death.

In these pages, I wrote what I felt, what my pen could write, and what I felt obliged to record.

# The Reborn

## Who Am I?

Although this is a simple question comprised of just six letters, many complicated ones lie behind it. These many questions have erected a mountain on my chest, preventing me from sleeping and causing me to wander aimlessly, lost in the pitch-black darkness.

*Who am I? Where did I come from? Why? Where am I going?*

These are fundamental questions for which philosophers and scientists have not found an answer. Poets, mystics, and sufis have long pondered about their nature.

These question marks have long battled with my mind, and urged me to worry and lose my focus, as though I were someone helplessly searching for water in a vast desert. I tried to forget it for a while, but it woke me up, screaming into my face:

"Who are you?"

"I'm Hasan," I would answer helplessly.

"That's obvious! Who are you?"

The idea of being known and unknown is one to contemplate. It makes me worry a lot at night and at dawn, when I hear whispers saying: *You are Hasan, George, Ahmed, Carl, David or Buddha... It doesn't matter. These are names you do not choose for yourself, you, human!*

"Where are you from?"

"I'm from Syria."

"It was mere chance to be born in Syria. Before you were born, you were neither Syrian, Eastern, nor Western. You were only a human being waiting for a way to Earth. Not the Moon or Mars. Your home is Earth."

I felt a bulk of pressure in my heart being lifted.

Yes, first and foremost, I am human. My first home was my mother's womb. My second is the Earth.

Then I was asked:

"What do you speak?"

"Arabic."

"We do not choose the languages we speak. Our communities offer us languages just as they offer us other traditions. But there is a common language inside us all. It is the language of emotions: joy, tragedy, tears, pain, and happiness. All humans share this language, and they laugh and cry in a similar way."

"I think people are different than me, and they might be hostile. They might become my enemies."

"Even you and your enemies are partners in pain and joy."

*As a Syrian poet once said:*

Do not burn your enemy!

Burn his hostility!

You and your enemy are from the same home

You all belong to Earth

You and your enemy are in love with one life

You are both partners in pain

You have blood of the same color

Your tears are mere colorless drops

You wear similar clothes in celebrations and funerals

You have both embarked on the journey in search of hope

You both pray for your daily bread, water, and air

You both have fragile skin, susceptible to fire

You both will die

Your mothers will wipe their tears on both graves

These tears belong to the same tragedy"

## The First Birth

I, like all people, was born once. However, I am different, as I was born a second time.

My mother gave birth to me the first time.

I was born the second time while observing the lives of those born at the edge of a homeland torn by a crazy war that tossed their shreds across all continents. I will discuss this second birth later, but now I want to talk about my first one.

I was born in some manner twenty years ago, in a town atop the Zawiya Mountain. Many stories lie behind the stones of this mountain, stories enfolded in history about dignity, about the man who refused humiliation to tarnish his reputation and cast a blemish upon his name.

Many legends and myths hide behind the rocks of Zawiya Mountain and in the warmth of its nights. Swallows and finches fly high and build nests in its trees.

It was in this region that I was raised, and, from my mother's bosom, I suckled the milky kindness of the breeze and the tainted beauty of the surrounding nature.

Oaks and laurel trees taught me self-respect and their leafy peaks implanted this sense of pride within. I learned how to be independent from these trees that covered me with their shadows.

This mountain, Zawiya, witnessed the sacrifices of martyrs who defended it against invaders. The stories of these sacrifices are hidden behind the trees and the rocks of mountain. You can still hear the whispers of heroic men who fought ferocious battles against the French army, resonating across the landscape.

One of the French generals described the period of the French mandate over Syria, while commenting on one of the battles they fought with the people of Mountain Zawiya:

"The battle with the rebels was difficult. Since the First World War, such a thing was unprecedented. They were about 150 men who nonetheless managed to break the French campaign. The rocks, the sky, and the rain fought with them."

## The Second Birth

I will remember this day as long as I am alive.

"Go to the water company and get a water tank to fill the swimming pool," my father said. I had been nagging over his head to fill my pool on a hot summery day. Swimming was my passion. I was seventeen years old.

My father was sitting absent-mindedly in his office, barely listening to my annoying adolescent requests. At the time, I thought he was busy with his business, trade papers and contracts. However, I do now acknowledge that I was wrong—he was thinking about issues more important than his business and money. Perhaps he was thinking of my brother, who had been injured by a stray bullet at a protest. The injury had prevented my brother from attending his last exam at university. We were hiding him in our farm without access to medical care. He might end up disabled for the rest of his life, but we had to keep him away from the police and its spies.

We are a big family. I have twelve brothers and two sisters, and perhaps our father was thinking about all of us. *While I was thinking about my desire to swim in cold water, my dad was anxiously thinking about the unknown, the near future lurking behind the door.*

At the time, he looked at me with his tired eyes and a neutral expression, addressing my nagging with a short sentence:

"Go to the water company and get a water tank to fill the pool."

My happiness at that moment was beyond imagination. I failed to notice his tone of voice or the way he spoke to me. Was he satisfied or disappointed? I did not think about it that day, but I am thinking about it now.

My life had been monotonous—divided between school and home. I had small dreams, and the biggest of them, at that moment, was to fill the pool and swim in the cold water.

I did not know this sentence would change the course of my life. I was surprised at the white hair that appeared on my scalp even before I reached the age of 20. That day, I travelled beyond the fabric of time and space to be born for the second time.

Every birth is accompanied by labor. We do not feel the pain of this process. Our mothers do. However, during my second birth, I felt and lived the pain of labor.

Now, I am more aware of the birth that changed my life hereafter, altering me from deep inside, exploding within my veins and flipping my brain folds upside down.

*The Reborn*

The turning point for my second birth came in the summer of 2011, a couple of months after the Syrian revolution had started in Daraa and spread across the country.

The Syrian people were gathering and protesting in an unprecedented uprising. The Syrian regime responded to the protesters with gunshots. It later escalated to the use of snipers to tanks, then fighter jets and barrel bombs.

Although I participated in demonstrations with my brothers and others in my hometown, I did not know what the people who were chanting "Freedom... Freedom... Peace... Peace, O' Daraa we are in solidarity with you!" wanted.

I was holding up my mobile phone to take photos of the protests, as photography was one of my passions.

*Day after day, the child inside me started disappearing. I was observing and thinking about what was going on around me. A new spirit occupied me.*

I wondered why bullets targeted people. They were protesting peacefully. They were not criminals.

These questions echoed inside me, and for the first time in my life, I saw tanks moving in my hometown.

I was distraught and full of strange feelings mixed with wonder: Why were these tanks arriving?

We used to draw tanks, and they would be fighting enemies: Were we enemies?

Death was looking out at us from their barrel bombs while they crushed the air.

## Naked Chests Against The Tanks

The day my older brother was injured became part of what shaped me during the process of my second birth.

People in my hometown used to protest on a daily basis. And on Fridays, there was a main protest after the prayer. It was the month of Ramadan. People were protesting in the hours before they ate their *iftar* meal, after sunset.

The first week of Ramadan was peaceful. While people marched in their protests, they passed near military checkpoints and armed soldiers. The regime's soldiers were ready to shoot, and they were looking carefully with fear behind their eyes, their heavy helmets hiding their heads and necks, while their fingers rested next to the triggers of their guns. As I chanted, I was secretly filming them. I was watching their eyes. They reflected happiness after the protests passed away peacefully, and we knew that the hearts of these soldiers were with the people. They had relatives in other provinces who were protesting against the dictatorial Syrian regime, and they liked what we did. Some of them were trying to escape or defect from the Syrian regime's army to protect the people, and some refused to kill.

Meanwhile, security forces were searching homes and arresting individuals who participated in the marches, so the protestors increased their demands: Freedom of those who have been arrested.

On the ninth day of Ramadan, the voices of the protestors were louder than usual, and there was rage intoxicating the air—a man and his child had been killed on their motorbike by a sniper stationed on a nearby hill..

When the protesters gathered that evening, the terrifying sound of that tank was buzzing in the surroundings, with its thick black smoke. They are still stuck in my memory.

"What's happening?"

Some of the protesters raised their voices. These were the relatives of the ones who had been killed. They were chanting and cursing the president and his ruling party. Three men lay in front of the tank, which seemed intent on swallowing people, trying to impede its wild treads.

The tank stopped, but unidentified gunfire sounded for a long time, and the furious people grew frightened. The gunfire continued. People asked for an ambulance to help the injured. With my mobile phone, I was filming the men who lay in front of the tank. I witnessed a horrible scene.

My brother was amongst those laying in front of the tank in pain, gripping his injured leg.

People rushed to rescue the injured, and I ran to my brother, crying and screaming. I was happy that he was alive. I was not sure who helped me lift him and put him in a car to take him back home. We could not move him to a hospital because security forces were trying to arrest him and put him in solitary confinement. They had done that to one of his colleagues.

My mother shared with me how worried her and my father were about us on that day. As she was preparing the *iftar* meal, her body was at home standing in the kitchen, but her soul was with us, and she had been growing absent-minded. In the evening, when she heard the voice of gunfire being shot at the protests near our home, she screamed: *My children! Oh God, save my children!*

Meanwhile, my dad shouted that they should open the door, might there be any injured protesters seeking refuge in our house.

Inside car that was carrying my brother home, I was sitting beside him. My t-shirt was dyed with his blood, and my tears stained his skin in return.

I wondered what was happening, and why....

My brother was in pain, for a bullet had hit his knee and was now gnawing at his flesh. How could we get it out? Where could we secretly get a doctor?

*That day, I knew we were not allowed to show our wounds. We had to be silent. We had to hide so we would not be arrested.*

We stood helpless in front of my brother's screams, waiting for the arrival of a dentist to help him. But this man did not have the courage to come and help. Thank God, though, a young nurse came and tried to stop the bleeding with a thick blanket. The dentists managed to give him a painkiller injection he hid in his pocket. The nurse could not fetch a first-aid bag,   as that would have drawn attention.

The nurse told us we would have to transfer my brother to a hospital, but on the way to the nearest hospital, there were several checkpoints set up by Assad's regime in order to arrest protestors who were ironically considered ¨elements deemed a threat to society, a destructive force of the country's stability, and a breach to its security; all arranged by the wit of wise leaders". And if any of the protestors got arrested, not even a blue fly would know where they would be taken. That is what I heard that night at home, and which I struggled to understand.

But, by some miracle, we managed to transfer my brother to the nearest city Maaret al-Numaan. We put him in a car with several women, and we passed through all the checkpoints. At the first checkpoint, a soldier wanted to check the car but one of the women told him "Shame on you! Get away! We have a pregnant woman". Another woman reiterated in a calmer manner, "My son, we have a woman about to give birth, and it is an emergency. Would it really matter if you check the car?"

The soldier apologized and went away.

The car then passed through other checkpoints, one after another, until it arrived at the final one, which refused to allow the car to cross unless we paid them with two boxes of foreign cigarettes. The soldiers told us: "God help you. If you have a boy, come back and bring some sweets!"

Although my brother safely arrived at the hospital, his problems were not seemingly put to an end. During the three hours spent in the surgery room, the doctor always kept a worried eye at the door, fearing the security forces might ambush the hospital. If they did come, they would arrest everyone inside.

The bullet had shattered the bone, and my brother needed two metal plates affixed in his knee. There was only one brand new plate available, so the doctor ended up using another second-hand plate. The surgery was successful; however, my brother left with a permanent disability. I witnessed these horrible moments, while my brother was in pain, how his leg was encased in plaster. I can still hear his words mixed with complaint and worry resonating in my ears. "I want to go back to university, tomorrow is my last exam. I need it to graduate."

He failed to graduate.

That was one of the incidents that initiated and shaped the labor process of my second birth. It was followed by another incident that affected my parturition. It did not come with bullets, and it did not shed blood. This time the bullets were of a different kind. It was the words my school director used to talk about my brother's injury.

## A March of Love for The Dictator Killing His Own People

We were in the middle of the first class when the bell rang and we were asked to gather in the school square outside. Despite being shocked at first, we were later happy to leave our studies and get out of class, albeit, our happiness was transient. A whisper struck my ear:

"Maybe the security forces have come to arrest the students who participated in the demonstrations!"

My heart began thrumming with fear, as I have already heard stories about the security forces' methods of arrest and torture: the ghost, the tire, the flying carpet. I thought they would come to arrest me, as many had seen me taking photos and filming at the demonstrations.

On the stairs between my classroom and the square, I lived long moments of terror that lasted for centuries. With every step, I imagined myself blindfolded, walking through dark basement hallways to reach a torture cell, its walls painted with blood and, behind its bars, several savage monsters were waiting to eat my soft meat.

When I reached the iron fencing that separated our classroom from the square, I remembered the story of the young man who was injured alongside my brother, one of three men who lay in front of the tank. His story had reached our house, and people said that he was arrested at the hospital, before the doctor managed to examine him, and no one was allowed to treat his wounds. He was bleeding while they transported him to the Idlib Central Prison, where he was put in solitary confinement for days before another prisoner was allowed to help him, not out of compassion. The forces did not want him to die, they would lose torture material.

That was the reason my family hid my brother for more than three months, even from our nearest neighbors.

Once we had gathered in the school courtyard, my eyes searched for the soldiers who would appear at any moment to arrest me. The school director shouted, ordering us to shut up and listen closely to what he was going to say. We forced ourselves to listen to his husky voice.

As usual, he said a lot of things about the homeland; patriotism, loving our leader. He warned against outside factors who wanted to destroy our country, and praised the 'great' reformations that had been implemented by Mr. President.

I knew that most of the people in the country hated him, the students for one set of reasons, and the adults for another. I didn't know at that time why people said that he was a missionary for Shia Islam and in contact with Iran, and that he was paying 100,000 Syrian pounds for those who converted to Shiism.

Anyway, on that day, the director ended his speech by saying that we had to get on the busses moving to Idlib to take part in the march in loving support of the leader. His words hit me like a thunderbolt. What sort of love and loyalty was he talking about?

Yesterday, the leader's soldiers shot my brother and his friends. They even killed another boy in my class, one of the kindest and most polite of all the students. I felt the devil of stubbornness mounting to my shoulder and whispering inside my ears that have just been banging with fear a while ago. I told myself I won't go to the march.

The director kept repeating his threats, trying to convince us that we should do this out of love for the leader. He said it was our choice to participate, yet, he also waved the card of harsh penalties to face all abstainers, including school expulsion. He repeated that we must go out of our own free will, and no one would be forced to go.

Despite all these threats hanging over my head, I left the others on the way out of school, under the pretext of going to a restaurant to get a sandwich. I stayed there until the march proceeded upon the path of love and loyalty to the soldiers who shot my brother. At the time, I did not think of the consequences, but the others went away, and no one noticed who was missing and who was marching.

Day by day, the population of the village thinned. The arrests began to alarm the villagers, and people felt they were living in a prison. Security forces spent nights searching for the leaders amongst the protesters and those called "sprayers" who sprayed anti-regime slogans on street walls. My mother and brothers gained the habit of sleeping with their clothes on. My father was afraid security forces would come and break down the door as they searched for my brothers, particularly my injured brother. His intuition was right. That horrible night, we heard a violent knocking at the door before the sun dawned upon us with its warmth.

## Night Raid

We were shaken from our deep slumber in and woke up terror. However, it was not a lonely knock after which silence ensued. It was rather followed by a series of bangs that sounded like the machine gun fire we used to hear tearing through the darkness, night after night. Rapid footsteps were moving around the house and under the windows. The rough voices stabbed at my eardrums as I sat in an inner room with my injured brother. I heard a loud voice threatening to break down the door.

My father opened the door and asked: What do you want? I understood that they wanted to search the house, and my father was asking them to wait until the women were warned, but the sounds of their boots were already filling the house. It was only a matter of seconds until they entered our room. They stared at my brother, who sat in his bed, his injured leg covered with a blanket.

They asked us to show our IDs while they checked and overturned everything: furniture, pillows, table covers, and drawers… Meanwhile, my father gathered our IDs and gave them to the senior officer who stood in the salon. The men turned everything in our home upside down, particularly the books we had stacked on the shelves, flipping through each and every page.

*The Reborn*

I heard a man's voice asking my father about his name and surname more than once. My father kept on answering with a composed manner. The inquirer raised his voice and told him to be sure of his answers, and my father said again:

"Is there anyone who does not know their own name? Our IDs are in your hand, you can check them."

A long silence followed, after which the senior officer told his men in the salon, to leave after they have searched every corner, including the crawlspace above the bathroom.

In the end, the senior officer apologized to my father, calm now, as if he were not the same man who has just been shouting.

"We apologize," he said. "We received information about terrorists who had names similar to yours. As you know, we are keen on maintaining the security of the country, and your security and safety as well."

I heard my father utter a few indistinct words before he closed the door behind them.

"What happened?" we asked our father, circling around him.

"Some son of a bitch reported on us, and they came to arrest us."

"So why didn't they?"

"God saved us and blinded their eyes. Some wicked snitch told them about your injured brother, but fortunately they did not notice his injury with his leg covered by the blanket."

"But they checked our IDs and read our names."

*The Reborn*

"Yes. It was our names on our ID cards that saved us."

"But how?" we asked, surprised.

"It seems those who reported us only knew the names people call us, but not the ones written on our IDs. They thought we were not the same family they were looking for, but they will surely be back tomorrow after that son of a bitch confirms this is the right house. We have to leave."

And so my father has decided, saying firmly that our town was no longer safe for us to live in. That we were lucky this time, but we might not be that fortunate the next.

My father wasn't the only one making this sort of decision. In the face of these night raids, the entire village was now facing such terror. The distances between security checkpoints shrank, and your ID card was almost never in your pocket between your home and the market, and on other daily errands. Gradually, the people from the mountain began to flee as arrests increased, and deaths doled out by the regime snipers who hid on the roofs of tall buildings.

My family was one of those that fled from Zawiya Mountain, which regained its strength of memory. Those who remained fought the regime forces, and were as tough as the mountain and its oak trees. It was one of the first spots in Syria to defeat regime forces, even though the regime used all kinds of weapons including Sukhoi fighter jets, MiGs fighter aircrafts and helicopters dropping barrel bombs that burned the mountain, driving out more people to save their own lives and the lives of their children.

Thousands fled into the open with their loved ones, in search of safety.

And so it was that my family moved to our farm in Khan al-Asal, located on the outskirts of Aleppo filled with scattered farms and luxury buildings where people used to spend the summer and holidays. Those fancy farmsteads were mostly for businessmen and expatriates, but they did not come that summer, as the smell of death spread from the fires of Syria.

We began to worry about our far-flung family, and we welcomed and hosted more than one of our relatives, or those fleeing from our mountain hometown.

I heard my father calling the owners of the empty farms to get their permission to host those who had fled their homes. For the most part, they were welcoming, and they agreed to help no matter what the situation was.

I also heard that many people could not manage to find safe a place, so they went to the Turkish borders, hoping they might be granted asylum.

## On The Edge Of The Homeland

At times, I would remember my father's words:

"Go to the water company and get a tank of water to fill the swimming pool."

I feel the letters of these words slapping me awake from a deep sleep, triggering storms of the painful memories that we lived in the country. His words bring back all the woe I saw in the faces of those who came to our farm seeking shelter.

I went to the water company that fill swimming pools in the farms, and I asked for a tank from someone we knew.

I do not know why all these details boil inside me, as I sit next to the driver who got me a full tank of water that jostled inside. I could not wait to fill the pool to escape the summer heat inside the cool water.

I was lost and confused, and I felt almost guilty for not identifying with the pains of others. I think my father, when he gave me his consent, was well aware of this, and knew all these painful details. On the way with the tank in my lap, I noticed a big truck passing close full of women, men, children, and some assorted furniture and blankets.

On the faces of the children who were crammed into the bed of the truck, under the searing heat of the summer sun, I read a tragedy the universe could not absorb.

They were new migrants, doubtlessly having fled from death. They left everything behind: their homes, their memories, their school friends, and perhaps even the graves of their loved ones, surviving with what remained on their bodies.

But where would they go after they have lost everything?

As if I asked the question aloud, the driver answered:

"May God help them! They are on their way to the Turkish border. There, they will live in the open air under the burning sun. The lucky ones will find olive trees to shelter under, but they will live without food or water."

The word water fell like a barrel bomb on my ears: "Without water?"

*The Reborn*

"They stand in queues for long hours to slake their thirst. Some of my colleagues went there, and the greedy ones among them exploit their need for water."

"They sell them water?"

"Yes. But there are some who fear God and send free tanks of water."

How ashamed I felt! I wished the ground would crack open and swallow me, I who had taken a tank of water to fill the swimming pool and play in it.

I remembered the people who had escaped from Zawiya Mountain, leaving everything behind. I also remembered those who came to our farm seeking shelter and a safe haven. I reminded myself of their stories and the stories I heard about them. Their words were mixed with tears, loss, destitution, and broken spirits.

I remembered the stories of children who could not carry their small toys along, after cuddling with them every night on their soft pillow under a safe roof and a warm blanket.

When we drove past the truck full of migrants, I saw a child holding a cage with a bird inside. I could not see the bird very well, but it was large and looked like a pigeon.

At that moment, I do not know how I remembered the story of the phoenix that I was told as a child. I remembered its details I watched the face of the child who was holding his birdcage between piles of children sitting on the swaying truck that moved next to us. I do not remember whom I imagined as the phoenix. Was it myself? Or those children?

## The Phoenix

As my grandfather said:

"Once upon a time, a long time ago, there was a bird living in paradise called the phoenix. It was similar in size to an eagle. Its color was fiery gold, and feathers ringed its head like a crown. Its wings were larger than those of an ordinary eagle, and they were so soft as to be angelic. The feathers of its long tail were red and orange, and became yellow when it traveled long distances. When it was more than a thousand years old, and had gained great celestial powers and wisdom, it wanted to go down to the earth to see how people lived, and to share their hopes and joys. And so, this millennial bird made its way from heaven to earth, crossing oceans, mountains, and valleys until it smelled the cedar trees and pine resin in the mountains of Lebanon. There, it built its nest on the peak of a cedar tree, using frankincense, myrrh, and ambergris. In the morning, when the threads of dawn first appeared, the phoenix saw a sunrise, the beauty of which had never been matched in any of its journeys. It began singing heavenly songs with its angelic voice resonating in the sky.

When the guardian of the sun heard this voice, he rode up on his wagon pulled by four fiery horses to express gratitude. At the phoenix's request, he showed him the pain of people and their tragedies. The guardian of the sun showed the phoenix a vivid picture of life on earth. The millennial bird screamed with rage and pain as it felt the tragedies and injustice among the peoples. The phoenix beat its wings inside the nest such that the ambergris sent out sparks and lightning. The horses were so afraid they struck it with their hooves, and sparks scattered onto the nest, enough to burn the bird within. The bird did not leave its nest, but rather chose to stay in solidarity with people. With their pain and suffering.

Thus, the phoenix turned into ash. Yet, this was not the end of this bewitching mystery. It was merely the beginning. An egg appeared under the dust, its crusty white shell shimmering under the grimy ashes. On the first day, the egg grew bigger. On the second day, two wings emerged.

On the third day, the phoenix was alive. It carried its nest of frankincense and flew to the city of the sun, Baalbeck, before it flew back to heaven. Yet it preferred to come back and die cradled in the cedars of Lebanon rather than staying in paradise forever. This is what happened every 500 springs, or perhaps a bit more. The phoenix died and was resurrected from its own ashes".

* * *

Without thinking, I told the driver:

"Go to the border."

Surprised, he asked, "To where?"

"To wherever the people who need water gather."

"I do not know those places. I have not went there before."

I spoke in a way that was entirely new to me. "We will ask, and we will not give up."

The driver hesitated. "I heard that they are near a village called Atma, but it's quite far I think."

*The Reborn*

I tried to persuade him with the same passionate urgency I had used on my father, hours before while asking him to fill the swimming pool. "Listen! I will double your fees and will also offer you a satisfying bonus, God willing. You will also be rewarded by God if we give water to these people who left their homes and everything they owned."

Again, the driver hesitated.

"Yes, you are right, but the company will miss me, and there is more than one customer waiting for water to fill their swimming pools."

Urgently, I assured him we would not be late, and that when we come back, lunch would be my treat: a luscious barbecue together on our farm.

The driver finally surrendered in the face of my insistence, or perhaps to my enticing offers, and said:

"There is no power or strength except in God, and God knows best." Then he extended his arm to the gearshift and doubled his speed, following the truck full of migrants.

I told him he was right, the truck was most likely going to the border.

We continued our way in silence, and it was longer than we had thought—more than sixty kilometers. The driver almost wanted to change his mind, saying that people were waiting for their turn to have their swimming pools filled, but I reminded him that our mission was more important and noble, as displaced people needed us more than those spendthrifts who did not feel the pain of others. I did not mention that, a few hours before, I had been one of them when I went into my father's office, begging him to fill my swimming pool. That was the day I was born for the second time, six years ago. Since then, I have lived with those who are drowning in sufferance, with every detail of their pain.

When the crowds of people appeared to us in the distance, it was not as I had expected. I had an image of endless rows of blue tents stretched out, as previously seen on television.

In reality, people were scattered here and there between the olive groves. I saw blankets and sheets, quilts and mats, all hung on the trees so the elderly and children could sit beneath them, with some tents that appeared to be well-kept in front of which were tattered, dirty blankets. We passed by more than one family that only had olive branches' mercy. To my surprise, I failed to notice the protest behind us, calling to us from afar. Dozens of women, men, and children ran behind, begging us to stop. They were holding containers, utensils, and jugs. I then asked the driver to stop in what I guessed to be the middle of the clusters of people surrounding us. The driver slowed his vehicle, asking through the window for people to move away from the tires, repeating:

"There is no power or strength except in God. May God avenge this injustice."

My happiness that day was like nothing I have ever felt before.

Every drop of water that was poured into the vessels of the thirsty was a balm for my soul. It quenched a deep thirst within me such as I had not felt, especially when children who sat before their mothers prayed to us that God would quench our thirst with holy water from the well of Zamzam and from the heavenly basin of Morod, on the Day of Judgment.

*I did not choose my name or nation or religion. I found all of that ready-made, but on that day, I chose.* That choice changed the direction of my life entirely, as I decided to be with those people, especially with the children.

*I chose to live their pain, not to imagine it. I chose to touch their tears—not to describe them from afar, but to taste their salt, and to warm my frozen spirit with their heat. I chose to live with them all the details of their lives, and to leave the good life I enjoyed. I decided to dive and sink into their sorrows and tragedies, not into the pool of our farm, so that I might find a bright crooked smile hiding beneath all their dark tears, or I myself draw one on their lips.*

That day, instead of swimming, I enjoyed being with the children, sinking our bare feet in the mud puddles that formed around the hose.

* * *

What sin had these children committed as to be denied the basic amenities of a decent life, be it their schooling or even one droplet of water to quench their thirsty innocent souls?

These questions buzzed in my head as I watched the children's defiance, their chants, their begging and their prayers.

"Oh ammo (sir), may God help you and protect you, may He protect your children, please pour us a little water. We are so thirsty."

I heard another, pleading:

"My father is injured and we have no water."

I walked up to him—he was not more than six years old, and he was barefoot and wearing dirty clothes. He pulled up his sleeves and plunged into the mud to reach the source of the water located between the legs of the adults.

"Where is your father?"

Without hesitation, he pointed to the olive groves.

"There, under a big tree."

I took the container he was holding and filled it with water, but it was heavier than his small body could carry. I lifted it for him and said:

"Walk in front of me and show me the way."

He tried to convince me that he could manage carrying the container, but I refused, so he hurried to walk in front of me and guide me to his family.

We approached the large tree to which he had pointed. There was no tent, but only a blanket hung to block the sunlight. In the shadow, I saw a woman in black squatting next to a man in his forties who lay on the dirt.

The woman stood in surprise when she saw me, hurrying to take the container from me and expressing her gratitude and prayers for me. I told her not to thank me, as it was my duty, and of this sentence I meant every letter. I approached the man who was moaning beneath the tree. I asked after him, leaning close to his head.

"Goodness, God willing."

The man opened his eyes, trying to answer me with a murmur. He was unable to express himself, and thus gave up and closed his eyes.

*The Reborn*

"As you see," the woman said, "he is injured. Yesterday, he was wounded by a bullet in his shoulder". I noticed that his upper torso was covered with piles of bloodstained rags.

"What are you waiting for, auntie?" I asked in surprise, remembering my brother on the day he got injured, and the pangs of pain he suffered from.

As the woman spoke, she was trying to give him a sip of water, although her hands trembled and more poured out of the sides of his mouth than he drank.

"We are waiting for him to be able to enter Turkey. We are waiting for our turn. They told us today…there is nothing to do but wait."

I found that, like her, I was helpless, and yet this made me even more determined to find a solution for the afflicted.

Before the body of this man and his suffering, I forgot myself, and his pain merged with my brother's who lay injured in our home, hiding from the eyes of informers and government spies.

I forgot the driver of the tank for whom people were waiting to fill their pools, I forgot that my parents would worry about me and start searching for me, thinking I might have been arrested or kidnapped, and that the driver's family might also accuse mine for his disappearance, since he was on his way to our farm.

I did not even think about the reaction of my father whose consent to pursue this road I was not granted. But he did nothing apparently…

*The Reborn*

When we returned around six in the evening, five hours after we had set out, they had already searched everywhere for me. I told them about everything that had happened, and I watched my father's eyes, waiting for his response.

He neither punish me, nor did he even raise his voice. He did not praise my good deed either, but only said:

"You should have told me."

Yet I read in his eyes a satisfaction with what I have done.

\* \* \*

Images of the displaced along the borders of our homeland, amongst the olive trees, behind blankets and sheets…. remained with me in those long nights, and still have not disappeared. I can still taste the eagerness of the barefoot children as they ran after me asking for a droplet of water. I can still feel their soft feet pushing at my ribs, just as they splashed in the mud around the tank, as I slip my body under the sheets. .

I can still hear the groaning of the injured man who waited under the olive tree for an ambulance to carry him to a Turkish hospital repeatedly buzzing inside my ear, just as the face of his wife, full of tears of defeat, never left my mind. These many images were enough to drive sleep away from my eyes. I sat awake until the dawn call to prayer.

What happened to the people I saw? What happened to the injured man I met? Was anyone listening to his groans under the olive tree, or did he become a martyr of his wounds? Had those who were thirsty gotten enough water?

*The Reborn*

As these questions swelled, I felt ropes wrapping tightly around my neck and choking every breath from my being.

Where were these homeless people fed, if at all, out in the open? How did the children sleep when they were starving? What would be the fates of these thousands of people who lost everything and had no shelter except the sky and trees and some tattered sheets?

I could not sleep as those images raced before my eyes: the groaning of the man, the tears of the woman who could do nothing to help, the bare feet of children in the mud, their begging and dirty clothes. I remembered, imagined and dreamt of many things, all of which flowed into the idea of helping those people.

This was the first time in my life that I witnessed such misery with my own eyes.

Nights passed before those questions carried away me from my warm bed to the labyrinthine lives of the displaced. I found myself among them again, *deciding to live with them, to share their lives and try to make their voices heard in the world. Yes, I decided to be the hand of the disabled and the voice of those who were suffocating.*

Yet, convincing my family, and especially my mother, was no easy task. I started by trying to convince my family that my injured brother had to go to the border to enter Turkey with others who were injured, as his leg could not heal properly in the difficult conditions of the field hospitals. My parents were convinced, and I'd hoped to go with him, but they decided to send him with our relatives who had easy access to the borders. We later lost contact with them, as their mobiles had only Syrian chips.

*The Reborn*

Yet I did not lose hope of following them. I insisted on catching up with him, or at least waiting for him at the border, and I made one argument after another until I managed to convince them to let me travel.

\* \* \*

Only a few days separated my first adventure with the water tank from the second in a series of not-so-fortunate-events. Before anything else, I aimed at seeing the homeless whose images had been engraved in my eyelids. I remembered them as I stared through the window of the car that sped with me toward the border. I did not see the summer landscape beyond the window, a screen reflecting the time spent in the past few days. I felt my weakness as an individual, and feared I would not be able to meet the needs and demands of all those people. I thought about young people like myself, who believed that this move was temporary, and it would be just a few days before they would return to their towns and cities. Indeed, some of them joined me in helping the crowds, gathering what was necessary, and delivering it to these good people.

Day after day, with patience and determination, the dream became a reality.

I found myself there, on the border between Syria and Turkey, among those who were truly lost. I came to the border, carrying my dream to help the children who emerged from the fire and offer them the wings of the phoenix. The phoenix that was resurrected from its ashes to fly anew and forever.

Day after day, my team of volunteers grew in number. We had no idea about volunteering, or about how to cooperate with humanitarian NGOs. Our one and only goal was to help people—we became a bridge between humanitarian NGOs and those who were in need. We discovered a lot of people who were greedy and exploitative of the situation of the weak. We made mistakes sometimes, but with the help of God, we managed to overcome them.

Some mistakes were the result of people's greed, and others were the result of the ignorance of NGO workers who neither understood Syrian people's culture and customs, nor their social and religious traditions. Since we were these people's native citizens, we were better able to help and meet their needs.

But our first concern was, and still is, the children.

We dreamt, and still dream, of helping our children fly away from the scorching Syrian fire. These children are our treasure, and all that is left to us from our homeland. They are the hope to resurrect the Syrian phoenix after the fire has passed.

*We started there, behind the trenches. Behind which hid those thirsty for their own names and faces, and hungry for air, bread, and water. There behind the trenches where also hid those thirsty for the blood and sweat of slaves— those who guarded the walls of prisons and the dungeons of spirits.*

*We started from there, where death flowed like rain and the sky was heavy with tragedy; where ruined roofs collapsed, leaving people without shelter or enough live on; where human values were being shed like blood.*

While we were helping people on the border, we were also spreading inside the country, sharing people's tragedies and the goals behind their primary demonstrations.

For the first time, I felt that I have found myself. I found myself here, where tents multiplied, crammed with children's eyes and the images of corpses, massacres, and rubble; resonating with the sound of car bombs interrupting sleep and the noise of jets carrying barrel bombs, cluster bombs, and rockets. The tents where the winds of loss, destitution, and deprivation howled with the memories of the dead of yesterday, and the sorrows of tomorrow, of those children condemned to death before bearing the light of day, and young people who lost their dreams forever.

During these days, I felt the tents were a booby-trap, an earthquake jeopardizing the indifferent world above that has long lost its conscience and went into deep slumber.

*From there, behind trenches, where a story was woven for every tear and a novel was written for every drop of blood; I tried to write objectively, using colorless tears and bloodshot redness that pertain to all humans, to all life stories.*

*Everyone should know that no matter how many stories of tears and blood there were in Syria, no matter how diverse the heroes and characters were, they were all eventually spilled into one character and one story of grief. Syria was the story, and the sound of its pain travelled to fill every corner of the earth. The world must help us rescue those who remain alive, especially the children and young people. Otherwise, the horrible images of pain and bloody violence, which penetrated deep within our younger generations, will undoubtedly cause a mental crisis. These images have formed a growing memory that could be dangerous, a dynamo that might push humans to show their dark side—committing crimes or worse—and, in this case, it will be not only Syria paying the price, but the world in its entirety.*

\* \* \*

I wrote in my notebook:

I started from here, inside the heart of violence that has torn apart my community, especially the lives of children, and has broken apart the structures of social, educational, and moral life, rendering the fabric of society lifeless.

I believe if Syrians had continued their peaceful protests, the dictatorial regime would have fallen because tanks could not have persisted in the face of olive branches. But day after day, the regime pushed people to carry the arms filling its caves of death—aircraft and missiles, heavy and light—and it was them who gave light weapons to those who had lost a dear one for vengeance. They said that, in the Friday demonstrations, the regime distributed weapons to some as to get filmed and show the world that it is the opposition troops amongst the Syrian peoples to have commenced carrying the weapons of war. The regime went even further and allowed some of those who protested near security points to besiege and kill some of its members, as to legitimize using force against other peaceful people. The regime also allowed other countries to send weapons across the country and join in the Syrian destruction plan.

# No Time For Joy

When I stepped out of the car that had taken me to Atma Camp, which was getting larger every day, the first thing I wanted to know was what had happened to that injured man who was laying under the olive tree.

Hundreds of concerns flooded into my mind as I stepped into the olive grove, and I tried to remember his exact location, but in vain. I tried to remember the shape of the olive tree that he had lain beneath, but all the olive trees looked the same. All the trees drooped with broken-hearted misery, their trunks heavy with the furrows of time. All of them were trying to raise their canopies high despite their age, while the branches swooned towards the ground with a strange longing. All of the trees somehow pitied the people who had found asylum nearby. Even the families beneath the trees were similar. I was searching and looking through the tail of my eye, afraid they would think I was eavesdropping on their private moments, but I could not find the family—I could not find a man who lay beside a weeping woman. I felt a twinge in my heart and asked myself:

"Is it possible they moved him to Turkey? Or did he die of his wounds? What did that poor woman do, alone, as she saw her husband take his final breath? Did he die of thirst, or did he drink some of the water I had brought him? Regret is squeezing my heart—I should have stayed by the woman's side and helped her."

I saw a child walking between the olive trees, moving from one to the next, stopping for a moment as if he was looking for something. Then he ran off into the trees, and I imagined he was the boy who carried water to the man. Without thinking, I ran quickly to catch up with him. I did not know his name. He seemed to be the boy I knew, of similar height and thin body, and he even wore the same clothes. Then he stopped, sensing I was following him. The features on his dirty face were similar, but he was trembling. What surprised me more was that, when I got close to him, he threw the empty plastic bottle he had been holding and squatted down, raising his palms as if he was trying to protect his face of a coming danger. Then he cried, begging:

"I swear to God, it wasn't me! I didn't do anything!

I walked up and tried to calm him down. "Come on, don't be scared."

I tried to be reassuring, but he kept sniffling, crying, and pleading with me:

"I swear to God I didn't do anything, I just lost my family and I'm looking for them."

Gently, I took the hand that hid his face and helped him stand up, murmuring to him: "Come on, buddy, I'll find your family."

When he calmed down a little and lowered his hands, I realized he was not the boy I have been searching for, although he had the same broken-spirited look in his eyes. I had forgotten that all the children carried the same sadness, humiliation, terror, and broken spirits. All of them wore the same dirty, soiled clothes. After all, where would they find water to wash their faces, let alone their clothes? These were the children I had seen in the crowds, desperate to fill a gallon of water.

The boy asked me a strange question: "You mean that you aren't going to take me to jail?"

I was surprised by the question, and whispered:

"No! Why should I take you to jail?"

"Because the army took my big brother Aziz when they saw him running." The boy examined my clothes, then asked:

"You're not from the army?"

"No, sweetheart, I'm your friend who's going to help you find your family. Who's with you from your family?"

"My mom and little brothers."

"Where's your dad?"

He stared at me, his expression turning grim. I regretted asking such a question, afraid he would say that his father was a martyr. His voice was strained as he answered:

"My father was hurt by the army, and my uncle took him to Turkey. My mom, little brothers and I came after him this afternoon, but we couldn't find him."

"Are you the biggest brother?"

"No, my brother Aziz is the oldest."

"How did they take your brother Aziz?"

*No Time For Joy*

"I saw them when they came to our house to search it. My brother Aziz got scared and ran away from them. They ran after him because he was running, and they grabbed him and took him away."

"They didn't release him?"

"They didn't return him for a week. My dad visited the army and managed to help release him, but my brother had been hit a lot and tortured, and after he was released, my dad sent Aziz to my uncle in Lebanon so he won't be arrested again."

Realizing why the boy was so frightened when I ran after him, I said:

"I'm not an army man. I'm your friend. Come with me and we'll look for your family."

Then the boy picked up his empty bottle. "My mom sent me to find water for my brothers."

I stretched my hand out to his small palm. "Come with me, and we'll find water for your family."

Before he gave me his hesitant hand, I noticed an uncomfortable look in his eyes.

"You're not in the army, right? So then why were you running after me?"

I felt confused. "There is no reason. I wanted to help you find your family... I knew you were lost ... Don't you remember anything that was near them?

He stayed silent, thinking for a while. "Next to the cars that go across the border."

43

He flicked his eyes from one place to another and then pointed. "There! No, no, no, it's there. No, there! I don't know…"

Then he turned to me, and a heavy tear ran from his eyes. He said, resigned, "I do not know."

"Next to cars?" I asked him, to be sure.

"A little away from the cars, under a big olive tree… Yes, Mama is waiting there for my uncle to come back from the hospital with my dad."

He almost cried as he showed me the empty bottle. "My brothers are thirsty."

I put my hand on his hair, petting his soft scalp. "Don't be scared. I'll take you to your family, and we'll find water for them, too."

He gave me his hand without looking at me, his eyes searching here and there.

I took his hand and his worry eased, reassurance seeping through his tensed body. I went with him from one family to another—he, looking for his family, and I looking for the family of the injured man of whom I found no trace.

I found a big jug of water beside a door of a tent made of rags. There was an old woman nearby, and I asked her permission to fill the child's empty bottle.

"Go on, my son, you're welcome," she said. "But please be careful not to spill any, because they haven't brought us water for two days now."

*No Time For Joy*

I filled the bottle with great care and gave it to the child, who put it directly on his mouth and drank its contents ferociously, as if he hadn't drunk for days. He drank nearly half of it while the old lady was staring.

"Oh my heart," she said. "How thirsty you are! May God not allow those who are behind these atrocities to be successful in their destructive endeavors. What sins have these children committed to be driven away from their homes?"

I wanted to thank her and leave, but she pointed to the bottle. "Fill it, my son! Fill the bottle and don't take it away empty. This is all from God's goodness and the goodness of our benefactors."

We went searching, and the child led me to different places until we grew tired. Hundreds of families were scattered under similar trees, in similar tents, with similar faces.

Then, suddenly, as if the boy who was holding my hand had been stung, he slipped away from my hand and started running, calling, **"Mama! Mama! I'm here!"**

There, I saw a middle-aged woman clad in a black dress, most of her face covered by a black scarf. She ran towards the boy, arms outstretched to hug him so that he almost disappeared in the folds of her black dress. Then she pulled back and started hitting him on the shoulder with anxious slaps. She shouted at him:

"Where did you run off to? You broke my heart! I have been looking for you for an hour. Oh God, did I need more problems in my life? God help me,

I'm tired! Isn't it enough that we don't know anything about your dad and your brother whom we forgot?"

She wept for a long time while the child escaped from her slaps and ran to hide behind my back. The woman looked at me with an apologetic gaze while I bent towards her, offering her water to drink.

"You're the one who found him? May God reward you with goodness, my son."

She stood up to her full height, her forty-something face wet with tears. With a trepid smile, she thanked me, mixing her gratitude with blame for her son Muhammed, as she called out to him.

Her words, through which I caught dripping grief, began to echo inside me:

"Oh Lord, bring me the relief of the grave, I'm so tired, Lord! An injured father who's between death and life, and a son whom we forgot in the village…"

Behind every sentence there was a story of pain.

When she saw the sweat dripping on my face, she motioned to the shadow of the olive tree nearby and told me, "Come and rest, my son." I found myself walking behind her without knowing why, and I forgot the family I had been looking for. There, under every olive tree, there was a new story. Under that tree, there was a story of Um Aziz.

\* \* \*

With my fingers, I brushed away the stones and made a soft place to sit between the three children and Muhammed, the oldest and the fourth amongst his siblings.

While they stared at me in silence, wondering about their sudden guest, they each stole the bottle of water from the next.

Meanwhile, Um Aziz did not wait for me to ask her: *How are you, auntie? Are you well, God willing?* Instead, she began sharing the painful story that was nearly choking her. She began talking to me as if she were trying to apologize for the exhaustion her boy had caused me, and I realized she wanted to vent out the oppressive grief inside her. She wanted to speak of the explosive pain of each of these details, buried like knives in her heart. Through her sentences were interrupted by her tears more than once, I managed to collect the strings of Um Aziz's story.

Abu Aziz was a man like many others—a simple worker in a race with the sun to feed his family, which was made up of five children and their mother. If he found work, they could eat. Otherwise, he would borrow that which would allow him to make ends meet for his family, although he rarely found someone who would accept lending him money.

He would wake up in the morning, leaving his children asleep, and ask for God's help with his livelihood:

"Oh God, the Supreme solution-maker, you know my situation!"

There was no work he refused. One day, he would work as a carpenter, making roofs from cement, while another he would work as a builder or painter. He could dig foundation holes for homes or even the holes for toilets.

He could also shift rocks or sand. His motto was: "There's no shame in work, and what's important is not to beg from people."

What was important to Abu Aziz was to come back home at the end of the day carrying bags of food. His children would be waiting in front of the door, shouting with happiness:

"Baba's back home!"

They would hug him, asking, "What have you brought us?"

Despite his severe exhaustion and his swollen muscles, which ached from lugging cement, he would play with them and carry them on his back, not minding their mother's shouts: "Kids, let your dad relax!"

"He said that their laughs made him forget his exhaustion," Um Aziz said. "It was rare for him to come home with nothing in his hands. He would bring things he'd promised to each of the children, even if he would work late in the night to secure their price."

She swallowed a bone of tears stuck in her trachea to continue with her story:

"Namir, my husband, made a living whatever the difficulties were, and he would fight for his living in a moral way.

But after the demonstrations started, everyone was busy with their fears and concerns about the fate awaiting them, thinking only of what they would eat and drink the next day. No one thought of building or painting their houses.

The workflow was frozen, and everyone said, 'May God protect us from what's coming and from its effects'.

Abu Aziz, like many others, could not eke out a daily living.

He would go out in the morning and come back at the end of the day, empty-handed, dragging his footsteps behind him. The sound of his children's voice ringing in his ears would almost paralyze him as he imagined them jumping around him, as usual, asking:

"Baba, what did you bring us?"

He would tell them:

"Tomorrow, darlings, God willing. Today, there wasn't any work."

And Um Aziz could feel her husband's pain as he answered them, and his increasing disappointment.

"Come on, children, your father is tired and he wants to relax."

But he would stay with them and say, with pain rasping in his throat:

"Tomorrow, God willing." Yet he knew, deep down, that tomorrow would not be a better day. It was one of those dark nights that were becoming increasingly oppressive, while the children were sleeping. Um Aziz walked into the bedroom. She walked to her husband carrying a pot of tea, steam rising from its mouth.

Abu Aziz loved tea to the extent of addiction, but that night he did not ask for tea because he knew the gas canister was empty, and there had been no gas in the village for more than a week as the gas pipelines were blocked. Even if gas were available, the gas canister would be expensive—more than four thousand Syrian pounds, which was the equivalent to four days' work—so he ate his food dry and plain and went back to the bedroom in silence.

He neither noticed her come in, nor did he see the teapot—he was leaning on his arm in silence, staring distractedly at the ceiling. She knew the magnitude of the concerns drowning him, and the increasing pressure debts laid on his chest, day after day.

She did not know how to read his silence. She was his beloved before being his wife for more than twenty years, but she feared his angry stubbornness. Yet, she was the only one in his head, and she never tired of trying to maneuver around his steadfastness if she wanted something.

She poured two glasses of tea, anxious of startling him from his absent-minded state:

"Drink the tea, Abu Aziz."

He stared at the glass and gave Um Aziz a wondering gaze. She understood and answered, "Did you think Um Aziz couldn't handle this? I can make tea appear from the underground below our feet."

She whispered, "God will relieve us, there is no obstacle without a solution."

He started drinking his tea as he continued slipping away in his sea of thoughts.

She moved her body next to him until her chest brushed against his arm, whispering warmly, "I'm going to suggest something, but don't get sad or angry."

He looked at her out of the corner of his eye. "Go on."

She hesitated a little, as she already knew his answer, but she started off by saying, "It seems that things here are bad, and will get worse with no hope for the better."

He sighed and said, "Unfortunately, that's the reality."

She was encouraged and went on. "These sons of bitches, I mean those at the military checkpoints, mess with people and try to humiliate them. If God wasn't taking care of Aziz, he would've gone and not come back."

She paused, leaving room for him to admit to what she just said. She knew his suffering each time he wanted to leave the village to work.

"Is it not like this?" she asked.

He sighed. "It is true. You know, if I hadn't brought with me the secretary of the Baath party branch here, and confirmed that Aziz never once protested, the bastard officer would not have let him go, and he even might have been transferred to Idlib. That's why they still hate me. Thank God now Aziz is with his uncles in Lebanon."

"There's no safety any more, isn't there?"

"My God, no. Yesterday, I had a good job—a thousand Syrian pounds for a few hours work—but they stopped me from getting out. They said there was tighter security now and a ban on leaving.

The officer at the checkpoint has been carrying a grudge against me ever since that day I asked him about Aziz … Oh God, it's like we're prisoners here."

She made use of this emotional moment and seized the opportunity to lay down on the table her proposition. "What do you think of leaving the country—immigrating like the rest?"

He rose up, as if he was struck on the back.

"What? Immigrate? Where to, God willing? If we leave the country for them it will become theirs and for those after them. No, my love, this is **our** country".

She pulled back a little, trying to give room to his emotions.

"I know, I know, my dear Abu Aziz. These are hard times and they will end and we will come back. There's a proverb that says: Stick to the place where you earn your living."

He heaved a long sigh at the word *living*, as though she just stabbed a finger at source of his pain. "But where should we go, Um Aziz? All the villages around us are in the same situation. Their livelihoods cut off—when there's work, shopkeepers won't notice the flies. But if there's no work and no customers, they'll try to kill and distract the flies around to fill their time. God help us! Where would we go?"

She was encouraged now to throw the bombshell she has been thinking about for a few days: "To Turkey, where we can get Aziz from Lebanon and live together."

He would have almost exploded in her face upon hearing such words, yet he knew what lay deep inside her—her heart burned with longing to see her darling son. So when she mentioned his name, he restrained and diluted his reaction as much as possible. "To Turkey? Will we leave our country and go to live in tents? I've heard about the people who live in camps on the border, and even those who got into Turkey. Have you heard how they live?"

The woman kept silent in the face of his anger, while he continued:

"The whole family is in one tent: the father, the mother, old and young children all crammed together. The tents are next to each other with no barriers between them except a thin cloth. That means when someone snores in the next tent, it sounds as if it's in your own. You have to queue up to go to toilet...so what do you think about this sort of life? Will you accept all this, and a basket of food once a month? Are you willing to live on charity, Um Aziz?

I spent my whole life working with blood and sweat to build this home and make a room for our sons and another room for our daughters, and I did not ask for help from anybody except God. Now you're suggesting we go to the camps and live in a tent where we would roast in the summer and drown in the winter, not to mention the wind that would snatch away the only roof we might have above our heads, and what's worse is we would depend on the humiliating charity of food baskets. What kind of life is this?"

Um Aziz realized, from the intensity of her husband's words, which almost woke the children in the next room, that there was no point in discussing the topic further that day, so she postponed her efforts. "May he who would humiliate you perish, oh master of men. Let's leave this for now."

"I will never leave my home and my country unless I'm dead, do you understand?"

*"I agree with you," she said. "Don't be angry, please. Dear God, I know you don't need any more problems. I wish I would have cut out my tongue before uttering these words."*

He felt the warmth of her words, so he kept his voice down and moved towards her.

"Don't worry. I won't leave you in need, not as long as I can stand on my feet. Tomorrow, God willing, I'll leave our town for the western neighborhood, regardless of the checkpoint. I'm going to work for Abu Rami--I'll sneak inside so that wicked general does not notice me."

"I know you'll be careful, my dear husband, but, may God protect you, don't risk your life. Those soldiers are children, and some of them have no fear of God, and they might shoot you."

\* \* \*

When Um Aziz told me the details of that Thursday night—the last night she spent with her husband—she confessed to me with tears interrupting her flow of thoughts, "I was probably the reason, and I wish my tongue had been cut out before I suggested the idea of leaving the country".

I asked her about what happened the next day.

"I don't know," she said. "I wasn't there at the checkpoint, and I still haven't seen him since his brother transferred him to a hospital before I arrived at the border. They told me everything I know, which is that my husband attacked the checkpoint to get out. Maybe I was the reason—he wanted to prove to me that he's a man capable of putting food in the mouths of his children no matter what.

Some of those who saw what happened told her:

"We were standing in a long queue in front of the military checkpoint, and soldiers were taking IDs and checking them. They allowed some through to go to their farms or orchards, and they ordered some back, saying it was forbidden. When it was Abu Aziz's turn the officer asked him:

'Where are you going?'

'To the western suburbs.'

'What for?'

'"I have work.'

'Work in western suburbs? Don't you know that there are terrorists there? And are you going there to work with them. Man, don't you understand? Are you an animal? Isn't it enough that we released your son who was protesting against us every day? And now you want to go out to that neighborhood?'

'It's forbidden!" the officer said. "Especially for you!'

The witnesses said that Abu Aziz kept calm in the beginning, and didn't raise his voice, but said quietly to the officer, 'Isn't it a shame to describe a man like me, who's the age of your father, as an animal?'

The officer answered sarcastically: 'It's not an honor to have a father like you. My father and officers like me protect their homeland. You only bring terrorists to destroy it.'

Abu Aziz paid no attention to this response and said firmly: 'I'm a construction worker, and I have children, and I must work to earn a living for them, despite you and your father who raised a disrespectful son as the one standing before me. Do you understand?'

'Watch your tongue. I can shoot you right here. We said it's forbidden and that's that.'

'What do you mean forbidden? Are we in prison? Are we detained?'

'Don't raise your voice at me. I have nothing to do with it, this is what the orders say.'

'Where do you get your orders? Take me to your superior and I'll tell him about disrespectful soldiers messing with people. Take me to your superior!'

'Our superior officer is sleeping, and he won't wake up before noon. Go away! People behind you are waiting, and you're blocking the queue.'

'I told you before that I'm not going to leave. I need to work.'

The witness said: "At that moment, loud voices meshed in the air and more than one soldier intervened. Even a lieutenant was trying to push Abu Aziz away, who approached the building where the superior officer slept. We don't know exactly what happened. All we know is that we heard Abu Aziz shouting, 'I will get out whatever you do!' Then we heard bullets, and after that we saw Abu Aziz lying down on the ground in a pool of blood. We ran toward him—the blood was gushing from his chest—and then we heard the lieutenant saying, 'Get him away from here before I kill him.'

An old man shouted at them: 'You are murderers! How could you shoot an unarmed civilian? Go and point your gun toward the border with Israel!'. And then the lieutenant pointed his gun at the old man and said, 'Get away from here before I do the same to you.'

"What happened next?"

"I was home," Um Aziz said, "and had no idea what was going on, when one of our relatives came up, shouting:

"'Um Aziz, gather your children and be ready to follow your husband quickly, before the army reaches your home.'"

She understood that her husband had been hit in the chest by a bullet, and that his older brother Omar helped him get an ambulance to the Turkish border. His family had to follow, as now he was a terrorist in in eyes of the army, and they might search his home and arrest the entire family. After that, Um Aziz wandered around the courtyard of her home without knowing what to do as the children cried around her. Half the village gathered in their home. They brought her a car and told her to get to the Turkish border before Abu Aziz, so they could enter together."

Um Aziz said that she didn't know how she found herself in a truck, and that more than one of those who defended Abu Aziz at the checkpoint clash got in the truck with her.

"With so many children around, I forgot one," she said. "I don't know how I forgot my son."

\* \* \*

When I first met Um Aziz, she had already been at the Atma refugee camp for nearly two hours. At the time, I did not know the details of her story, but I still remember how she was wandering crazily among the crowds of people who has escaped from death, looking for someone to help her. Even the people from her hometown who came along with her got lost in the crowds. When she checked on her children as she stepped out of the truck, she knew that she had forgotten little Rami. She asked more than once, "Boys, did you all come?". And they would all answer with a yes.

Anxiety about her husband's injury made her forgot everything else. She hoped to catch up with him before entering Turkey. Even that dream didn't come true, as he had entered already, and she had no choice except to wait like the thousands of people whose injured were inside Turkey while they sat at the crossing-point gate, watching the empty ambulances that returned full of the injured coming from the places in Syria where demonstrations had taken place.

But the situations of these people paled in comparison to that of Um Aziz, whose heart was broken into two pieces—one in Turkey with her husband, and the other with her son, whom she had forgotten in her hometown. She wanted to go back and search for him.

Here, I found that I could offer help to the woman, as I had spent nights alongside the pains of such people, and now finally there was someone who needed my help.

Without thinking, I said: "I'll help you, auntie."

She looked at me eagerly. "I hope you can, my son, but how?"

"I will go back with you to the town, get your little son, and then we will come back here and wait for your husband."

I knew she did not want her gaze to shift for a jiffy from the Turkish border crossing that might bring back her husband. At the same time, she was completely oblivious of her son's current situation.

*No Time For Joy*

Thus, I said to her, realizing how helpless she must be feeling at the moment, "Auntie, Abu Aziz, may God heal him, is in good hands, being treated in a hospital. And, as you said, he's with his brother."

She nodded, waiting for what I would say next.

"There's no point in waiting here. We have to go back to your town because your little boy will be there, waiting."

She wept. "Oh, my sweet boy, where will he be?"

I tried to comfort her. "He's fine, God willing. There's no doubt that relatives and neighbors offered him a safe place, and he must be there, waiting for you. We have to go back to the village."

Then I asked her, while trying to guess the time by looking at the sun's inclination and its shadow, "How far is your village?"

"About two hours by car."

"We'll get there before sunset," I said.

"But my son, listen, I can't go back and stay in that town without Abu Aziz. I'll come back here to wait for him. They will arrest us if we stay there."

"Don't worry," I said. "The important thing is to get to the boy before evening because moving around at night is hard, as you know."

\* \* \*

I felt very motivated: I was about to do something great for the first time in my life. I had a feeling that we would find the child, and that's what I told her as the taxi drove us and her three children to town.

*Later, I wrote in my notebook about that trip:*

The mother told me many fragments of her life story, as though she had known me for a long time. Sometimes, she told me the start of something, but didn't finish, as if I knew everything. As if there were no need to repeat what I already knew. She was crying and laughing at the same time. Her smile would mix with her burning tears while the children around us were frolicking in a different world of their own. They were laughing, especially the youngest one, who, in my opinion, was not yet four. But the oldest one, who was ten, would ask from time to time: "Mom, will dad come back? Is he OK?"

She looked at him with dry, desperate eyes, and he would keep silent for a while then go back to laughing with his brothers. *It was better for the children's soft hearts not to know the size of the pain that afflicted their mother's.*

We arrived in the village before sunset. The last checkpoint we passed through was the most difficult. Many checkpoints had been set up around the villages to prevent demonstrations from connecting. We drove around town to enter from a side road as not to catch the soldiers' attention. The driver advised us:

"If they ask you where you are coming from, tell them Idlib. Be careful not to mention the words *border* or *Turkey* or *Atma.*"

Um Aziz directed the driver to her home. She was doing okay, and then suddenly, as if a demon had touched her, she shouted: "Stop here, this is our house!"

And before the car had stopped completely, she opened the door and threw herself into the street, catching herself so she would not fall. Then she headed like a storm towards a building that was partially collapsed. We heard her shouting:

"Rami, Rami ... Where are you, Rami?"

We followed her. The wooden door was broken, and there were the rooms and a courtyard space with a small garden and a few torn flowers. She was in a room where part of the roof and the walls had collapsed, as though it had been hit by a bomb. She was digging up the rubble with her hands, screaming:

"Rami ! ...Rami ! "

I stared at the rubble, and it did not seem to me it was burying the corpse of a child. I tried to calm her, saying that it was impossible her child was there. She stared at her hands in surrender.

"Where did he go? He must have been injured and taken somewhere else...."

I searched around for any trace of blood and told her:

"Oh auntie, if he'd been injured, we would have seen some evidence of that. I'm sure he is with some of your relatives or neighbors." Suddenly, neighbors started entering, but not as many as I had expected. It seemed that most people have already left town. And the worst was that nobody who came in had seen the boy Rami.

Um Aziz wept and shouted: "Oh my angel, where did my boy go?"

*No Time For Joy*

Then she went back into the collapsed house and searched the rubble and rooms until she gave up, after more than an hour, collapsing beside the house's garden and weeping bitterly.

Apologetically, the driver said: "I need to go. I won't be able to drive the car at night, as it's not safe anymore."

Then most neighbors who were there left, calming her by saying that when bombs had fallen on the house, nobody was inside, and before that the soldiers had come and searched the house, breaking everything, but Rami was not even home.

Some volunteered to search for her child, promising her they would not sleep till they found him. Women from the neighborhood tried taking her to their homes, but she refused, yanking away and sitting, exhausted, on an old chair beside the wall. Darkness began to fill the air.

"Trust in God, auntie. We'll come back here in the morning. Whoever took him will bring him back."

"I'll wait for him here," she said.

She brought me a plastic mattress and pillow out of the ruins of her destructed house and sat on the chair.

"Relax, my son."

I threw my tired body on the ground. "God willing, they will bring back your son back," I said. "Have a rest."

I do not know how I slept that night—I was so exhausted that I kept staring at a hole in the wall carved by a bomb. But I still remember how, when

I woke up, I found her sitting on her chair just as I left her, her eyes fixated on the broken door as she waited for news about her child.

God was kind to her, as she did not have to wait long. At sunrise, a man brought her good news that calmed her searing heart.

The man said that a lost child had been found in the western neighborhood, and that they did not know about his family.

"It's Rami for sure," she said. "I want to go there."

"I tried to go," the man said. "But they have blocked the checkpoints leading to the town, and they won't open them before ten. I told someone to bring me the boy."

We started to count the seconds until the clock hands struck ten. I saw Um Aziz madly going out of the door as she saw a man arrive, pulling a child behind him.

I saw her drop to her knees, hug the child, and then rise and spin around, his head pressed against her chest as though she wanted him to enter her heart.

When I approached, I could not hold back my tears. When she saw me, she ran towards me and held me as well. I heard her laughing madly, and I felt her warm tears on my face. She thanked me, prayed to me, and kissed my head.

At that moment, I felt I was breathing life for the first time, that I have done what adults could not do. I felt I was the reason for the woman's happiness.

She kept on repeating her prayers for me.

*No Time For Joy*

"May the spirit of God make your mother delight in you," she said. It was the greatest prayer I have ever heard. It made me happy, and I felt that not only did I help this woman, but I had also done my mom a good deed.

Um Aziz's happiness did not last long. There was no room for happiness in the middle of the troubles the Syrians faced.

We breathed a sigh of relief as, by some miracle, we got out of town. We were far away from checkpoints, approaching nearby towns that were preparing for that Friday's protests.

I remembered the big demonstrations that ran through roads and villages to meet in the public squares of the big cities. I remembered the sit-ins, and the painters who spent their nights on ladders drawing placards with people's dreams and demands.

I also remembered how the people held their hands up together, waving olive branches while chanting, "Freedom, freedom… peace, peace."

Some were holding others on their shoulders as they chanted, and the people were like waves moving from the ground. Some women threw roses and rice, while other women were handing out water, so that the chanters could wet their throats.

I wanted to join, but when I looked at Umm Aziz's face hidden amidst her children's, with Rami on her lap, held against her chest as though he were a little baby, I saw her face features shift back to worry and distraction. I tried to talk to her but Rami spoke first.

"Where's daddy? I want my daddy."

*No Time For Joy*

But it seemed that, from the moment we arrived at the crossing where the injured enter Turkey, fate had already made an appointment with Rami's father. The ambulance was heading towards us from Turkish soil, and Um Aziz's soul seemed to know who was inside. She walked to the crossing as though hypnotized. I followed. She stood there like a statue, her movements numbed down to nothingness. The only part of Um Aziz that moved were her wide eyes, which tried to penetrate the arriving ambulance that had stopped nearby. A man stepped out of the car and one of the children beside me said that was his uncle.

"That's my uncle Omar, but where's my dad?" the child asked.

They ran toward the ambulance and I followed, fearing the news we would hear about their father. The child repeated his question: "Where's my dad?" The answer came when Um Aziz crammed her body into the car and screamed: "Oh my beloved Abu Aziz, why did you go and leave me?"

For the first time in my life, death was embodied in a man covered by a bag and lying only a few meters away from me. I went back, my heart pounding. My body seemed to have solidified into one piece. I walked away as not to hear the voice of this woman who, for the last two days, I have been trying to bring joy to. And now, when a smile had almost worked its way onto her face, it had been suffocated.

*There was no place or time for happiness. No time for joy.*

# Perfumes in Memory

## Basil Doesn't Wait

It was a long, difficult April day. Hundreds of families flowed toward us, fleeing from the death infesting conflict zones. They left everything. Their homes. Their martyrs. The graves of their families. They fled fearing for their lives. They reached the gathering point near the border, dreaming of a safe sky that didn't rain death, and a land where they can roam free from the threat of imprisonment. They were stressed and exhausted. They have looked death right in the eye, and now they have arrived with nothing but painful memories. The wealthy among them were those who managed to escape with all their children and a bag of clothes. These unarmed civilians did not find mercy from any quarter. They had escaped the fire showering them from both the regime and the opposition. They had escaped from "elephant" rockets, gas tanks and barrel bombs dropped by helicopters.

On that April day, even the sun showed no mercy—the scorching heat made us sweat from every pore as we welcomed the newcomers and distributed tents and blankets to replace their destroyed homes. We worked hard, using every iota of our remaining strength, especially that the clashes had intensified in the past few days, and more than one town in al-Ghab Valley has been captured by the "revolutionaries".

I heard the splashing words of a man hollering with anger:

"How do we benefit from this liberation as long as they, the revolutionaries, cannot protect us? Once they succeed at liberating the country, jets arrive spitting destruction above our heads. We end up running away, leaving everything behind. This regime does not fear God; it burns everything down."

Despite the huge influxes of displaced people, we managed to offer what they needed of food, drinks, and tents before evening.

Fatigue was gnawing at every inch of my body, only when I entered one of the empty tents and lay down on my back, did I manage to finally take a deep breath and taste immense relief surging through my veins. The more services I offered to the displaced, the better I felt, despite my physical exhaustion. I closed my eyes. A vision of the day softly crept under my eyelids as the summery breeze stroked my tired muscles.

I sank into children's tired faces. I heard the cries of hungry babies. I experienced mothers' panic. I tasted the tears of bereaved women, and the humiliation in men's eyes. I began to pluck out from my memory the pieces of stories I had heard that day. Everyone talked about their lives, but no one finished their story. One story was about a family whose sole breadwinner had been arrested. Another family lost their eldest child to the warp he never came back from the fighting borders. A third family was still mourning their child whom they buried in the house garden because they were afraid of putting him in the cemetery. Even cemeteries were not spared from the shelling, notably during funerals.

Only a few families reached the border with all their members, and barely a slim few of these managed to remain in sound mind, or body. Some lost their eyesight to shrapnel while others lost a leg to a barrel bomb that fell right next to their houses. Some lost a hand to an exploding bomb that chopped it off.

*Perfumes in Memory*

Fire from a landing bomb mutilated the beautiful visage of a girl in the bloom of her youth, leaving her with misshapen features. When I saw all of these scenes, I felt a blessing rarely acknowledged by normally living people. My body I was of sound body and could move my limbs; I can wake up in the morning whenever I want and breathe comfortably; I can see everything around me. Most people who haven't lived through wars don't recognize this blessing, and they will not fully taste it unless they live with those who have managed to escape and survive from the claws of destruction.

I, too, am one of these survivors. For I have succeeded in evading death the many times it tried reaping my soul.

\* \* \*

I don't know how and when I fell asleep that night. A fine line separated me from the realm of sleep, until my phone rang and disrupted my serenity. It was a friend of mine, a doctor working on the border area, informed me that a new batch of immigrants had just arrived from al-Ghab Valley, the Hama countryside, and other areas. He told me to contact our volunteer friends to take care of these people and offer them what they would need. I was sleeping in my clothes. Before I had gotten rid of the traces of sleep clinging to my skin, I found my legs taking me to the camp's square. There I asked my friends to follow me, a demand they catered to without tardiness.

If it weren't for the woman who resembled my mother with her body clad in darkness, there would have been nothing new to write that night. Stories cradled smaller stories. Faces painted with sadness. Broken eyes tainted with misery. Hungry children who clutch at the clothes of their mothers.

Babies who cried while digging at their mothers' bosoms in search of protective warmth.

There would've been nothing new in these scenes without that woman standing apart from the crowd.

I saw her in the darkness. She stood like my mother. Her posture. Her clothes.

As I approached her, my heart trembled while my brain asked itself "Did they bomb my family's house? Might they be here? Where are my brothers and father?"

My heart almost jumped from my ribcage until I caught a clear glimpse of the woman's features. She was not my mother. It was rather Um Ahmed.

She was holding a small bundle that looked like a child. Under the moonlight, it looked like a black bag with a green, smooth-leaved plant protruding from it, pressed to her chest.

Without knowing how, I found myself calling her "mother".

*When you work with victims of war, you have to be careful with every word you say, as some uttered words might mistakenly kill a soul that managed to survive a barrel bomb.*

Yet, months passed and I made one mistake after the other.

One day, I committed a grave mistake by saying, "Come here mother, why are you standing there alone?"

She whispered to me as though she were speaking from a different world, to another human being.

*Perfumes in Memory*

"Mother! O' mom, where are your mom?"

Then she said: "My son, I do not have children" and further pressed the pot with the basil plant to her chest.

Without hesitation, I replied, "We are all your children, mother. Come here, you must be tired. I will show you a place to relax in."

I was about to ask if she had relatives with her, but instead I said: "Do you have your things with you?"

"No," she said.

She had nothing but that pot of basil. She walked behind me in silence. I did not ask her anything. People like her, despite having the urge to speak at some point, undoubtedly do not want to hear questions buzzing above their heads. If she intended to keep silent, then all the questions in the world would not break her mute resolution. I guided her to an empty tent and asked her to rest until I came back with some food.

She refused, in the beginning, to occupy a tent by herself, since she saw people were still left in the open.

"Children are a priority. Whereas I am all alone."

She only accepted to stay alone in her tent after I succeeded in convincing her that everyone would have a place of their own to stay in, even though I knew there might not be enough tents for all the people.

Some refused to stay in a tent. They still dreamed of returning back home, and felt as though the tent would extend their exile period.

*Perfumes in Memory*

I came back after a while to find her sleeping with the pot balanced on her chest in a strange manner, as if she were holding a baby, and there was a branch of the plant running parallel to her nose. I was confused and wondered about the story behind the woman and her plant.

I was about to leave the tent when she woke up, scared, and sat up. "In the name of God, the most Merciful and the most Compassionate, who is here?"

She gazed at me, as though trying to remember where she was.

When she saw the bag on my back, she pointed at it.

"What do you have in your bag?" she asked.

"My stuff. A notebook, some pens, and a camera," I said.

"Are you a journalist?"

"No mother, I am the one who brought you to the tent a little while ago. I work here helping people who are in need."

"And why do you have a camera? You are a journalist. My son would have loved to become a journalist…"

I did not ask her where her son was. I knew the answer the moment she shifted her gaze to the basil and remained silent for a long time.

I told her "Rest mother. You must be tired. Do you need anything else before I go?". Without hesitation, she asked: "Do you have water?"

"Give me a few minutes and I will be back."

*Perfumes in Memory*

I went out, my mind busy with the fact that she must be quite thirsty. I searched through several tents and finally managed to bring her a bottle of water. I sat beside her, staring in surprise as she removed the bag that was covering the basil plant and caressed its withered leaves.

Then, instead of drinking, she started to pour the water into the pot, and the basil permeated the air with its scent. Tears began trickling down her cheeks.

Um Ahmed did not need questions as to tell me her story, for, the next day, she herself approached me: "Come here, my son. I want to tell you my story."

\* \* \*

Her story was mixed with tears, blood, and the scent of basil. It was a story of four martyrs—one of whom the history books might write about, while the other three will remain forgotten.

"More than 20 years ago," she said, "Radi and I got married after living a love story that the people of al-Ghab Valley never stopped chewing and talking about. My family and his did not approve our marriage, however, he married me despite it all. We are from different sects." She whispered in my ear with fearful eyes: "I am Sunni and my husband is Alawite."

She looked me in the eyes to see any reaction to her words, but her confession did not shock me one bit. There were many cases like hers. Us Syrians, diverse in our sects and religions, lived alongside each other, nothing but the bonds of love and care joining us. We ate together. We drank together. We worked in the same markets and lived in the same land. Few were those who stood against intermarriages. It is war that separated people from one another, and it was the warlords who tore open this wound.

Her voice pulled me out of my thoughts.

"He waited for me for ten years, and then we forced everyone to accept our marriage. He said that we could birth a clan of children, as I loved having many children. However, God did not give me a child in the first year, nor the second nor the third. We visited every doctor we knew, elderly sheikhs, and all shrines. We offered our sacrifices, sang our prayers, and raised our supplications to the heavens above. Five years passed…

Abu Ahmed, God have mercy upon his soul, was in love with flowers and roses. He would care for them as a father cared for his children. And, seeing through his eyes, I found myself falling in love with roses and flowers. We had about an acre of land, and I planted it with all kinds of flowers. I made a fence from tulips and a roof from jasmine pergolas. We raised flowers, taking care of them and caressing them. We would get drunk on their aroma and even kiss them goodnight. These plants were like our children, and every rose had a name. I spoke to them and they spoke to me. My home was a heaven full of all kinds of flowers. You do know that flowers have souls and they understand people. We forgot children for a while…".

Um Ahmad sighed and kept silent. I did not have the courage to interrupt her. Then she continued and said, in pain:

"But nothing compensates not having a child of our own. People told me about a sheikh who lived far away atop a mountain only the birds could reach. I did not tell Abu Ahmed about my plan. I went to see the sheikh, bringing a slaughtered sacrificial animal, as they told me to do.

God helped us, through him, and I became pregnant two months later. After six years of marriage, I had my son Ahmed".

She was silent again, and when I looked at her face, I saw her eyes were full of two giant teardrops from her burning heart, dripping slowly down her cheeks burnt by the scorching suns of time. She sighed and continued:

"My son Ahmed was more beautiful than all of flowers in our house. All the roses were jealous of him, some withered and died from their envy. You know, children naturally envy each other.

When the protests were kindled on the streets, Ahmed was ten years old back then. When Ahmed's father went to work for the last time, he kissed Ahmed, who was not yet eleven, and told him, "Take care of your mother, you are the man of the household when I am gone".

Abu Ahmad seemed to know that he was not coming back.

He has not returned to this day, and we do not know anything about him. Some say he was kidnapped by some militia, and others say he was detained or possibly dead. I don't know," she said. "For a year, Ahmed would ask me about his father and I would reply,

"He will be back, my son. He will be back."

In Abu Ahmed's absence, everything in our lives began to wither. The first thing was Ahmed's smile and his laughs, which used to fill our home with joy. Then the garden—the stemmed necks of our flowers started to bend, sensing they have become orphans. At first, I thought it was a lack of water, especially that a shortage was caused due to the destruction of the main water pipes. But I always bought water to ensure my plants never got thirsty, albeit, my efforts led to no avail. In their faded colors, I heard every day a different question: "Where is Abu Ahmed?'. He loved basil so much, may God have mercy upon his soul if he has died, or, if he lives, may God ensure his safe return.

One day, Ahmed came holding a black bag, 'Guess what I brought for you, the most beautiful mom on earth?'

Analyzing the shape of bag, I answered 'What?'

'Something my dad loves a lot, and he will be very happy about it when he comes back. And you also love it. Come on, try guessing.'

From the bag I could taste the smell of Abu Ahmed. I said jokingly, 'I don't know.'

He opened the bag and it was…".

She stretched a hand toward the basil and placed it next to her cheek. I thought she wants to smell it, but she started implanting kisses on the basil's crumpled soft leaves as tears jumped down the stem, accompanied by her choking sobs.

Details of Um Ahmad's story dug into my heart and burned in my blood. It felt as though steam was falling from my eyes. Still, I had a major question about her story lingering in mouth.

Where was her son Ahmed?

She looked into my eyes as if she had read what was on my mind.

"Ahmed had no legs. If he had legs, he could have ran to escape the barrel bomb, but I was…. It was my fault."

*Perfumes in Memory*

Her last sentence froze my tongue. What did she mean by saying that she was the reason? Why did Ahmed have no legs?

She made an effort to gather herself to continue her story.

"When the barrel bomb dropped onto the garden, two days after Ahmed bought me the basil, it cut apart all the flowers, as well as Ahmed's legs, right above the knees. His body was infested with shrapnel."

The barrel bomb left me half a child. I thanked God a thousand times that he left me at least half of Ahmed, as all of our neighbors' children who were playing with him in the garden died. The bomb shards mutilated their faces, we could not recognize the identity of either.

I took him to every field hospital, but their capacities were limited, since originally they were established by benefactors to serve people who would not want to risk going to regime-controlled areas for fear of arrest. However, God saved and healed Ahmed. He would now move around the house with his wheelchair as the floor squealed in woe yearning for his lively footsteps and childhood frolics".

I said to myself, "Thank God he was not killed. He survived a barrel bomb, but where is he now?".

And again, as if she were reading my mind, the strange woman gazed at my face with her wet eyes and continued:

"The first time he survived, because he had two legs and managed to run a few meters away, but the second time he wasn't able to flee. He couldn't move when he saw the barrel bomb dropping from the helicopter above him. I was at market, and I was the reason he was killed. If I had been beside him,

I could have taken him away and escaped. When I came back, I could not find one piece of my Ahmed so I can at least bid him farewell.

She cried bitterly, and more than one woman passing by the tent entered and tried to calm her, but alas. When Um Ahmed lost control over her senses, her body bickering and quivering like a slaughtered bird, I could not help but call my friend the doctor to give her a relaxant injection.

*  *  *

After that day, I crossed ways with Um Ahmad multiple times, whereby she would hug and kiss me like an affectionate mother every time I saw her. I smelled my mother in her, warmth, and the basil that wafted from her chest.

Once, I saw her beside the water tank that distributed water among the displaced. She was holding an unusually small container.

I asked her, jesting, "Don't you have anything bigger than this?"

She smiled. "I do, but this is enough for the basil, and if I bring a bigger container, I would have to wait for a long time in queue, and *basil does not wait.*"

"How about you drink," I said, "and I promise you I will get the water necessary for the basil every day." I recommended she set aside water for the basil daily in case she needed it.

Months passed, and I did not see Um Ahmed again. I was told she moved to a new camp that was made to cater to the doubling number of the displaced. This new camp was not far from the point where we first gathered

*Perfumes in Memory*

to welcome the displaced. Despite the many problems we were busy solving at our camp, I left in search of Um Ahmed.

I learned from the administrators that she lived with some of her relatives who had settled in the camp. When I arrived at her tent, I was told that she was sick. I asked them to tell her my name. As they were entering her tent, I was surprised to see Um Ahmed running towards me. She pulled my hair, punishing me for my lack of communication and my absence while her relatives looked on in surprise. They watched her with eyes full of pity, especially when she called me "Ahmed" instead of my name. She guided me to the tent, and, ironically, she was smiling. Her smile was wide and bitter, a phenomenon I could not comprehend,

"Don't you know? Don't you know?? Come with me and I will show you."

She pulled me by the hand, pointing to the corner of the tent. "Look!" she said. "It's gone!"

In the corner, beside a mattress and pillow, I saw it.

It was in its black pot, its soft branches extended with their nakedness. The plant was utterly dry from life.

"You see, there is no basil any more, it is dead. It left me … all the martyred have left me… Ahmed went to his father, and the basil also followed them. while I stay here…"

All of us who were present had no language with which to reply to Um Ahmed's words, except with warm tears trickling down our puzzled faces.

\* \* \*

I wrote in my notebook:

*Many are the martyrs who are forgotten by history. Who would remember a basil plant withering in the midst of a bloody war? It was martyred by the lack of water, and its death killed in turn the heart of a mother. A bereaved mother who breathed from its smell and reminisced the traces of her long-gone beloved ones.*

# When will my fingers grow?

Birds? Or young boys laughing

like water flowing from a stone?

And their bare feet

Seashells chiming within a waterwheel,

The hems of their dishdashas like the northern breeze

Traveling at night across a field of ripe wheat

Or the hissing of bread baking on a holiday,

Or a mother murmuring her newborn's name,

Cuddling him on his first day.

Birds? Or young boys laughing

like water flowing from a stone?

- Badr Shakir Al Sayyab, "Arms and the Children". Dr. Terri DeYoung

I often remember the words of this poem, and chant them subconsciously, especially when I pass by those children playing and jumping between the tents, their laughter filling the world in spite of the misery, poverty, and deprivation reflected in their features. How correct was al-Sayyab when he imagined children's laughter as water flowing from a stone! He was capable of envisioning the future's light through their features of misery.

On that day, as I was passing behind some tents and a group of children playing with marbles, their voices grew loud into a fight. But one child, sitting apart from them, attracted my attention, so I headed over to see him. He could not have been more than seven years old.

This child was holding a jug of water, pouring droplets onto the dry soil. At first, I thought he was making mud to play with, as we used to do when we were children to build houses, sculptures, and toys from mud. The boy, however, was not making mud—he was playing a strange game, and he was so immersed in his game he did not notice my presence.

I came closer and stood behind him, observing his strange game. His right hand was planted in the soil right above his fingers. He surrounded his planted hand with a hole similar to the irrigation holes we made around flowers. He would, from time to time, pouring water in the holes around his fingers, waiting for the thirsty ground to absorb it before he would go on pouring again. Then he would wait, his eyes fixed on his planted hand until the water dried, and the game continued along this pattern.

What was this boy doing? What game was he playing?

I could not remain silent as such standing behind him, so I asked the child about the nature of his game. Surprised, he flinched at the sound of my voice coming from behind his back.

"What are you doing, sweetheart?"

He turned toward me in surprise without pulling out his hand from the soil. He put his left finger to his lips, as though asking me to keep silent.

I remained silent for a while, and then said "I want to play this lovely game with you."

*When will my fingers grow?*

"I'm not playing," he said. "I'm doing an experiment."

I asked in surprise: "An experiment?"

"Yes, our science teacher taught me this in school, and I'm trying it." Then he returned his gaze to his planted palm while pouring more water.

"Maybe the teacher lied to us," he said to himself.

"Can I help you?" I asked.

He looked into my eyes and nodded without changing his posture.

"Tell me about your experiment and I'll help you."

He started to explain as he looked at me. "The science teacher said that seeds will grow if they're buried in the soil and watered. Is that true?"

"Yes!" I said.

"She also said if we get a branch from a rosebush and plant it, it will grow and become a complete rosebush again. Is that true?"

"Yes!" I said, agreeing again.

Then he said, stubbornly, "No! It's not true! I've been trying for an hour now, and my fingers have not grown back."

In the beginning, I didn't understand what he meant. But when he pulled his right hand from the soil and held it in front of my face, I was shocked. I finally understood what he meant, wishing I did not entertain my curiosity.

His four fingers had been amputated, only his palm remained. I have seen many disabilities and injuries among the survivors, many of whom

*When will my fingers grow?*

were children who lost limbs, but the hand of that child sliced through my heart like a knife. The image of his hand in front of my face shall forever remain sculpted in the backdoors of my memory.

"Why didn't my fingers grow? Why does it hurt every time I pour water in the dirt? I can take pain, but why did the teacher lie to me?"

I had no answer to his last question. He went on while looking at the boys who were playing.

"I want to play marbles with them, but they wouldn't let me and they said I can only play with them when my fingers grow. How can I play without fingers? Even the teacher was mad at me when she saw me writing with my left hand even though I'm a really good student. When I told the teacher that the doll I found in the street exploded in my hand and took my fingers away, she cried and said that they would grow back again, God willing."

Suddenly, the boy started crying and asked me, over and over: "Why are my fingers cut off? Why?"

I felt his tear-filled eyes were directing the question at me.

"Is the teacher a liar?"

What can I tell you, little one? This war has blown up millions of questions like yours. We are no longer able to know the truth from falsehood, but I know that the only true thing is pain, and the truest is your pain and the pain of the thousands of children who will live their lives with permanent disabilities. Forgive me, little one, I am too small to answer you.

\* \* \*

*When will my fingers grow?*

That night, I wrote in my notebook:

I could not answer you, little one, when your eyes poured pain into mine. Maybe I can be more honest and open up to the pages of my notebook.

Oh, if only you knew, little one, how I wished I had no eyes to see all of this cruelty on the earth, inflicted by so-called human beings.

Oh, if only you knew, little one, how I wished to lose the blessing of my eyesight, so I could never see how humans use children as firewood to keep on feeding their wars.

Oh, if only you knew, little one, how I wished sometimes to lose my mind as not to comprehend all this ugly madness. I wish I were not aware, I wish I did not acknowledge the misery surrounding me. I am exhausted by what I see, by what I know, by what I experience.

Little one, you do not know what is going on around you. You belong to neither fighting party, but it is you and all the other children who pay the highest price. An elderly man who lost his hand might live with the pain for the few remaining years of his life, but children like you might live with the pain for the entirety of their lives.

Children are the only ones who are not responsible for war, and they are the ones who are most burned by its raging fires.

One fighter drops a rocket over a child while another drops a bomb that looks like a doll. Does that fighter have any children awaiting his return, expecting gifts and dolls?

*When will my fingers grow?*

What kind of heart does he have? Does a heart between his ribs even exist? If he might own such an organ, from what type of stone is it manufactured?

Indeed, I was too small, a dwarf before your pain, oh little one.

This feeling of helplessness is too painful that it diminishes my humanity. I am paralyzed by my inability to relieve your pain, or the pain of any child injured by our mad wars.

How awful it is to feel unable to help. We have no choice but to mourn, or weep like children, or to condemn, condemn, condemn. While adults continue to kill without justification.

It kills me when I stand helpless, unable to offer a safe haven for children like you—a refuge where the earth's angels can sleep peacefully, far from the horrors of war.

Do you know, my little child, when we were children of your age, we wanted to reach adulthood so quickly, but when we became adults, we again wished to be children as not to feel all this pain we see without being able to do anything?

Adults are the ones who destroyed the beauty of this life. Those like you, little one, are the most beautiful treasures the universe can ever offer us.

Ah, how I imagine a planet free from adults, filled with nothing but meadows of flowers and butterflies fluttering around your flamboyant bodies malleable as the wind.

*When will my fingers grow?*

If only adults leave this life because we are the ones who filled your eyes with black ashes, and let them bleed with the tears of agony.

It is 4:15 a.m., and I am writing to you. Tears trickling down my cheeks, I sense pain gnawing silently at my heart. Ironically it is not anger that fills my chest with heated rage.

I wonder, dear reader:

Does anyone else feel your loss, pain or sadness? They only watch from afar, don't they?

The feeling that covers your skin when you hear the scream of your newborn baby is unfathomable by human language.

Perhaps your father's feeling about your arrival in this life is bigger than your feeling about the arrival of your own newborn.

Have you ever thought what might the man who kills children feel, he who ends his mission to go back to the child waiting the boxes of toys and bags of sweets?

Does this fighter think of how the mother of the murdered child will feel, while he plays with his own in the backyard?

How could he plant a bullet in one chest while sowing joy in that of his own child?

Day after day, this tragedy grows bigger than our imagination, bigger than our plans for the future to come.

One day, after the chaos of the injured at the Turkish border ended, I tried—along with some friends and a volunteer doctor—to create a point of

*When will my fingers grow?*

contact and documentation for the injured entering Turkish hospitals through the humanitarian crossing adjacent to the camps. Our goal was to make sure families would not lose contact with their injured across the border. We were the link connecting hospitals and families together. The weight of work was bigger than we could bear, and my notebook was not large enough to document all of the injuries. In a few months, we managed to document a few thousand injuries, including a few hundred injuries whose owners were unidentified, left alone with no companions.

\* \* \*

How difficult it was to answer the inquiries of bereaved families.

One night, a child called to me, "Uncle, is my dad okay?"

"He is okay, sweetheart," I said. "In the morning, he'll be better."

Before morning, I had received news of his death. The child called out to me again, "Uncle, hasn't my dad come back?"

Words are of no use here. Day after day, we found ourselves unable to continue working in our offices. So, I went wandering in streets, scanning the façade of every office scattered alongside the pavement:

Orphan Care Center

Office on Missing Persons

Wheelchair Center

Center for Prosthetics and Artificial Limbs

Travel and Immigration Center

*When will my fingers grow?*

I searched a long time, but I did not find any sign saying "Hope Center for the Return of Refugees". It seems that our tragic story will continue down its path into the unknown.

# The Strange Grave

Have even the graves chosen to leave? These earthly smelling boxes we thought would protect the remains of those we love....

When I saw him for the first time in the refugee reception camp, anxiety attacked me. He said that he has been searching for me for quite a while. Some people led him to me, saying I could help him.

I looked at him carefully, searching for signs of his arrival from regime-controlled areas. He seemed in his thirties, short and thin. His cheeks were hollow, as though carved by the claws of a severe famine. There were bags of exhaustion underneath his eyes, creased with dark wrinkles. His cigarette always dangling at the corner of his mouth as he spoke.

I asked him: "How can I help you?"

"Finding my mother... I 've been searching in vain for the last four days. We've been separated for nine months now, with no means of communication connecting us. It seems she lost my mobile number, but what I surely know is that she must have come here."

"Who told you that she would be here? Why did she leave alone, without you going with her? How could you let your mom travel unaccompanied to the liberated area while you stayed in the regime-controlled one?"

Perhaps I was hard on him that day, addressing him as if he were a spy sent by the regime's security forces to report on what was happening at the borders, prying to collect the names of the staff and record people's

*The Strange Grave*

conversations. This would not be an unusual thing for the security forces to do. More than one aid worker was caught disguised as an informant for the regime, sending information about future bombing targets. Yet, the regime did not really need such information, as the bombing was usually indiscriminate.

Later, I would regret my hastily judgmental thoughts about him. Most suspicions are indeed a sin. On that day, he did not answer my accusatory questions, trying to hide his tear-filled eyes from me "You're right… But if you knew my story, you might excuse me, brother… Can you help me find my mother?"

His broken voice touched something deep inside my chest, some sort of pity directed at his helplessness. I changed my tone and said,

"Did you see the officials in charge of the camps?"

"I've been asking them for four days," he said.

"I'm not going to hide from you the fact that it's not easy to find your mom, especially if she doesn't have a mobile phone. There are more than 60 camps and in every camp, there are 200 tents. There are other camps as well in Qah and Atmah—amounting in total to more than 100 camps."

"I have to find her, even if I shall search the camps tent by tent. I've been dreaming about getting to her for nine months and eighteen days now. I have to find her."

"Why this long delay?," I asked, shocked at his ability to remain nonchalant about his mother's situation for almost ten months.

*The Strange Grave*

"I promise you, brother, it's a long story, and if you honor me by visiting my tent, I'll tell you all its details."

Curiosity promised him to visit that evening.

He greeted me in front of his tent, insisting that I enter first. He introduced me to his wife, who was veiled, while his daughter looked at me with fear and curiosity. When I tried to pat the daughter's head, she escaped and hid behind her mother. The wife welcomed me and prepared tea at her husband's request. But I refused, saying I neither drink tea nor coffee. I knew people's situations were tough. There was nothing in the tent except for basic furniture and a huge bag. When the man saw me looking at the bag, he said in a regretful tone:

"When we escaped from the houses we spent our whole lives building, the only thing we managed to get was our clothes."

"You are safe," I said, to express solidarity, "and this is what matters now, brother. Thank God for your safety."

He continued in a high voice: "I swear I don't regret anything, money comes and goes. All I want, God knows, is to find that old woman, my mom."

"We'll find her, God willing," I said.

"When she left Aleppo, she called me and said she arrived in a place called Atmah, and after that I couldn't get in touch with her again."

Before I managed to formulate a question, he sighed.

"Our story is long, brother," he said. "I will tell you all the details."

91

*The Strange Grave*

He then took the tea from his wife who was hidden so that nothing could be seen beneath her black cover except for her shining eyes. Then he said, "Let's drink tea and I'll tell you everything".

While drinking tea in the hot dry breeze, Abu Mary began to tell his story about displacement and loss.

* * *

"Before I got married, people called me 'Abu Maryam, in reference to my mother. My mom never called me by my name either. She called me Abu Saleh ever since I was a child. Her dream was to get me married and see my son whom she wanted to name Saleh, after my father, may he rest in peace. He died when I was a child.

She was twenty-five years old, devoting her best years to raising me. She suffered a lot to take good care of me, and had a hard time with her family and relatives. She didn't abandon me and did her utmost best to offer me a good life. She even worked in other people's homes to pay for my education. I studied at an agricultural institute. Even though I could've studied agricultural engineering at Aleppo University, that institute was better. The program's duration was shorter, so it would be easier for my mom to covering my expenses. After I graduated, to my mother's satisfaction, I was hired as an official in a poultry company. It was thanks to my mother's prayers that I got the job through connections of mine. Some of the others who graduated along with me went more than 10 years without finding a job. Maybe that's why I made sure to protect my job and take care not to lose it— but I didn't realize my mistake until the job cost me my mom. I got married and put myself in debt to buy a small two-bedroom home. One room was for me and my wife, and the other was for my mom, who was so happy despite it all. My mom would ask me in the morning, laughing: 'When are you going to bring me a son called Saleh?'

I joked with her, saying: 'We want to have a Maryam'.

After two years, my wife gave birth to our daughter, Maryam."

He then gestured toward Maryam.

"Maryam's now three years old. She was born at the beginning of the revolution, before Aleppo became involved in the uprising.

Day after day, the siege tightened its grip around our necks. Prices rose crazily and many basic foods couldn't be found. People started complaining. Meanwhile, the first demonstrations kicked off at Aleppo University and some other neighborhoods, while the regime's mercenaries, or the *shabbiha*, violently suppressed the demonstrations. Some of these *shabbiha* were released from regime prisons and given unlimited authorization to face down protestors, not to mention the military checkpoints backed by tanks and scattered across all the streets and alleys.

We then started to hear about people dying at the crossing points every day as they tried to secretly carry bread for their families from liberated areas into regime-controlled ones. The area called *Hal* Market in Aleppo was a cross-point and frontline observed by regime's snipers. When the war reached our neighborhood, many bombs were dropped nearby us, destroying adjacent homes but mistaken our home. Many were martyred, while the remaining few migrated to safer areas. My mom asked me to leave as well: 'My son, life gave me you and your daughter, so let's leave this country'.

"'Mom, where will we go?' I replied, even though I had been thinking of moving for quite a while, especially that the military might recruit me to serve in the army. 'Is there a safe place? They say that the war will last for a long time.'

I was thinking about my job. I was thinking about how to sacrifice my job, which was my sole source of income. But I was also saying to myself: This war won't last long, and I don't have to decide quickly, like my colleagues who left their jobs and immigrated to Turkey, or overseas to Europe. Some families with children became food for sharks in the sea, and I didn't have the spirit of adventure. I was born lazy and don't like change or new things.

As things in Syria escalated, and the corner of our home was hit, destroying half of the kitchen, I found myself searching for another area that would be safer."

I interrupted him, asking, "In the area controlled by the regime?"

"Of course—how could I live in the liberated areas? How could I cross to my job when the crossings are separated by hundreds of checkpoints? I might be stopped and questioned, not to mention the snipers atop buildings who would not even let a cat cross the street. They said that snipers were automatons that monitored movements in the street, such that people put up barriers of rags and other stuff to prevent themselves from being seen when they needed to venture past the crossing points.

Our rent was exactly half my salary, and we managed with the other half to live in deprivation and austerity until the end of the month, with the addition of some food aid received from some humanitarian organizations. My wife was living in horror, worried from the moment I went to work until I come back. What made it worse was when rumors began spreading that the regime would recruit those under forty years to serve as backup in the army. My mother went crazy and could not sleep or rest as she tried to convince me to leave the country, day and night.

I still remember our last conversation. I told her, 'Oh, mom, I'm afraid we wouldn't be able to live if I left my job'.

She stormed off, screaming as though I were a small boy who didn't know what to do. She said, 'Oh son, our living is ensured by God, not by you or the government. God never create a living being without giving them enough to live on.' She cried her heart off and broke my heart. 'When your father died,' she said, 'you were a year and half old, and we had nothing. But we managed to buy enough to eat from his work. He died, may God have mercy upon him, but God did not abandon us. We did not die. Our living came to our door.'

And then she changed her tone and begged me, saying: 'Oh son, please, let's move and go to the liberated areas. All your uncles have gone, and also the rest of our relatives. It's a tough time, but things will change and we'll come back."

Then, she started to cry. I heard her say, 'I don't want to lose you like I lost your father. I have no one to rely on in life but you and your children. This girl cannot live in horror, with the sound of the bombs that destroyed the cities nearby. Your wife is pregnant and, God willing, she will bear us Saleh, and the sound of one bomb might lead her to miscarry and lose the baby. Oh son, here no one knows what's going to happen'.

I thought calmly about her words. It was convincing enough to make me think about migrating. My salary was not enough even for the rent. It was no longer enough for a home that lacked life's basic needs, especially water and electricity. I started thinking about how to get out of Aleppo that was under siege. How could we cross the regime's checkpoints to enter the liberated areas? At that point, I started contacting my friends who had entered Turkey or crossed into Europe. I made a decision that made my mom happy: 'Tomorrow,' I told her, 'we will leave for the Turkish borders. From there, some friends will take care of us and help us with the next steps'.

I told myself, *'It's a beautiful feeling to pack your bags, to change your current place of living and renew your soul—but not to be displaced from your homeland away from everything you've built all your life, nothing but the unknown waiting for you behind the door'.*

I chose a day off, along with another family from our acquaintances, and we headed to the last checkpoint that separates us from the liberated area to the north. We prepared our sophisticated plan based on my mother's ID, which shows she was born in a town north of Aleppo. We arrived at the checkpoint, and I don't deny that the soldier, who spoke with a Bedouin accent, was polite to us, especially when he saw the children and women who were with us. By we, I mean my mom, my wife, my daughter and I. He said, 'A visit at this time, people? Even the madman doesn't leave his home these days'. I pulled the soldier aside and started to explain the lie I made up

*The Strange Grave*

the night before. 'My mother, as you see, is sick, and they told her that her father is on his deathbed, and he wants to see her before he passes away.

He replied, 'My brother, I understand you, but the area is full of terrorists and bombs everywhere. And you have with you women and children'. I told him that I worked as a government official and would not spend more than a few hours on the visit. I thought telling him about my work would help, but, on the contrary, it brought me more problems, since an officer overheard our talk, and he asked me, 'Are you really a governmental official?'

'Yes.'

'And you're willing to enter terrorist areas?'

I felt the accusation in his tone.

'Do you have a passport?' he asked, and I said 'yes' without realizing it was a mistake to say that, as the passport was my only way to get to Europe. He ordered me, 'Give me the passport!'

He took my passport, and, without looking at it, he shouted at me:

'I'll let the old woman go visit her family, but we'll keep your passport with us until your mother comes back. As for you, go to work and don't put yourself in danger!'

His words were firm, leaving no possibility to argue. When he saw we were unsure, he said, 'Make your decision and tell me.'

We were in a position where we couldn't think, so I hastily decided to wait for her. I might've made a mistake, I don't know. Maybe my love for my mother, and my desire to get her away from the bad life we were living was the reason I did what I did. My decision was that my mom would go with the people we know and I would give her my mobile number so we could stay in touch. She would go ahead to the border, while my wife and I would find a human trafficker to help us reach the liberated areas for some amount of money after I'd come back to get my passport. I was in a state of trance. I convinced my mother to go with the two old women, even though she refused. I told her that I would follow her the next day, with the help of some human trafficker, and I'd be going through difficult roads that required a lot of walking that my mom couldn't bear. I told her to go and tell me about where she would end up, and then I would follow her. I didn't realize how foolish I'd been until I got home that evening and found the house empty. I listened to her voice that night, calling from a strange mobile number. She told me that she'd arrived with the family in an area called Atmah, and she was waiting for me there. It was the only time she called me. I called the number again, and someone told me that she'd used his number to call, but he had not seen her after that. I don't know whether she was in danger or whether she'd lost the number I wrote down for her. One day, I started to insist that the soldiers at the checkpoint, who'd confiscated my passport, give it back. On the second, third, and fourth days they refused, and asked me to leave politely. But on the fifth day, the officer was annoyed, and instead of saying, 'Go away' he called a solider 'Take him and do your duty, so that he and others can learn a lesson'.

I spent several hours in jail, and the blood on its walls was enough for me not to go back again. They hit me with their hands and military boots, and the hours seemed like months for me. I still have scars from their whiplashes. If I hadn't been a governmental official, they wouldn't have released me."

*The Strange Grave*

Then he sighed painfully and put his head between his knees, thinking he would cry. As usual, I didn't urge him to talk. Then I heard him say, "For nine months I was in besieged Aleppo. God witnessed and knows that I tried all possible means to get out. I didn't think of my passport, which I'd left with the soldiers. I waited nine months and 18 days, and I only managed to get out four days ago, after I'd paid more than a thousand dollars to checkpoint soldiers and human traffickers. I spent everything I had, and I was even forced to sell my wife's bracelets and our wedding ring in order to reach this point, passing through death, destruction and burnt military equipment and cars."

His words not something I heard for the first time, and maybe he had exaggerated some points. But when he showed me the scars from the whips that left black burn lines on his back, I decided to help him as much as I could.

We spent ten days searching for Maryam, but we didn't find her. We searched all the encampments and contacted all the friends who worked with me in the entrances to the camps. Searching for a woman named Maryam turned out to be a mistake, as she'd used another name when she entered the camp.

According to her son, she'd used a second name, a name her husband had called her. That's what he told me when I met him on Aqrabat Hill for the last time. This place overlooks all the camps and the Turkish town of Ryehanli. This is where Maryam's son would sit at the end of every long day of searching through thousands of tents, scanning the crowds of the displaced. "No doubt my mom's in one of these tents in front of me, and I'll find her tomorrow," he'd say.

*The Strange Grave*

And, when I saw him the last time, he said, "I've found her."

He said that as he sat on the hill, his knees pressed against his chest, his chin resting on his legs. His eyes were full of tears. But happiness seemed to enter my heart.

"Really, you found her!? Where is she? When?"

He continued the story that he'd started in the tent, and his voice sounded as though it were coming from a faraway corridor, mixed with old rotten pain.

"A few days ago. She wasn't far from us," he said, pointing to the tents scattered on both sides of a wide street.

"Yesterday evening, I came back from the camps, disappointed as usual, and nobody mentioned anything about my mom. I sat down on the hill, looking for a new place to search the next day. But while we were sitting here, I caught sight of a funeral. It was a poor one, and in attendance were only a few men and three women—not more than that. I don't know why my heart felt something, maybe because it seemed like a poor funeral, or maybe because her soul was looking for me amongst the few people walking behind her. I found myself going down the hill and running toward her. When I arrived, they were moving her toward the main door and then to the cemetery that was for those who don't have graves. I smelled my mom. I swear it was her smell that I'd known for thirty years. The smell seeped out of the wooden coffin on the men's shoulders. I asked an old woman who was crying and stumbling behind the funeral, trying to catch up with the others:

"'Whose funeral is it?'

*The Strange Grave*

"She was the only woman out of the thousands of people who gave me the answer I'd been waiting for. She was a strange woman with no relatives, and my heart goes out to her,' the woman said.

"What was her name?" I asked.

"Maryomah," she said.

That was the name my grandfather called her with. Now I know why no one could help me when I asked about her, since we were searching for 'Maryam.' Then I screamed without knowing what to do, my voice echoing between all the camps: 'Mom! Mommmmmmm! That is my mom!'. The men who were holding the coffin froze, stopping when they saw me leap forward to reach it. They unshouldered it and put the coffin down.

"Let me see her, please, this is my mother."

A bearded man came up to me and said, 'My son, everything is the will of God, God gives and God takes away. Come here and be sure that she is your mother'.

When he moved the cover off her face, I saw the face that I'd been dreaming of seeing for the past nine months. She was my mom. I felt she opened her half-closed eyes and gave me an affectionate, accusatory smile. I whispered to her, "Mother, it's me, I found you, and I'll never leave you again'.

I felt her say that I was too late, and I shouted, pleading, "Mama, I brought you my son Saleh so you could see him. Saleh is a good boy'. But she didn't open her eyes. And then the bearded man drew me aside, asking me to be patient.

*The Strange Grave*

\* \* \*

Abu Saleh gazed at me with tearful eyes and whispered, "I've found her, my friend. I've found her, but it's too late. The old woman who was following the funeral was her neighbor for months and she said that my mom was waiting for me for a long time, and her eyes were always staring at the door of the tent and the street leading to the main gate, until she became sick ten days before. She couldn't get out the door, so she'd been sleeping at the doorstep. In her last days, her vision wasn't clear enough to recognize those who were coming from outside, so she was depending on me, saying every time she saw the shadow of a person, 'Take a look for me! Is that Abu Saleh coming?'. She imagined that all people knew Abu Saleh. The old woman said she'd tell my mom, while laughing, 'Would I know him if I see him?'. My mother would answer, 'He's so handsome, with a beautiful girl called Maryam like a moon beside him. Is there a small girl beside that man who's coming?'. She said that when they brought her food at noon, but she would hide it and say, 'I'll wait for Abu Saleh— there's no doubt he'll come today.' She'd often go to sleep hungry. The woman also told me, 'Your mother left me something for you'.

"What is it?" I asked curiously.

Abu Saleh gazed at me with tearful eyes as he pulled some green wool fabric from his pocket and showed it to me.

"This is what my mom left."

"What is it?" I asked again.

When he stretched out the cloth, I knew it was wool socks, like the socks my own mother made by hand on winter nights for my brothers' children.

He put the socks on his knees and stroked them.

"She made a pair of socks and a hat for Saleh before he was born. She told her neighbor that winter would be cold and Saleh's feet would feel it, so she asked the neighbor to bring a ball of wool and knitting needles to make him some socks and a hat". I saw red spots on the socks, and Abu Saleh stroked them. When I asked about them, he said that they were drops of his mother's blood, as her vision wasn't perfect and she would injure herself while knitting and the needles would dig into her fingers. Then he gazed off past me, staring far away.

"What would you think if I call my son Maryam?"

I gave him a surprised look. "Maryam is a woman's name—a name for a girl, not a boy. Also your daughter's name is Maryam."

He said without looking at me,

"But my mom was Maryam, and she was a woman with a heart of seventy men."

I remained silent. All the words in the world couldn't help me. I tried to change the topic of conversation. Failing to detour the subject, I asked, "Where did you bury your mom?".

"Where can we bury her? Do we, the displaced, have graves? If I had a choice, I would bury her beside my dad. Her wish was to be buried next to him."

*The Strange Grave*

Then he turned toward me and sighed. We, my friend, have not only lost our homeland that kept us together with our beloved ones, but we also lost the graves that reminded us of those we loved. I buried my mom in a strange land, in an unknown grave."

Then he added, kindly: "What I want form you, my friend, is to help me find the tent where she lived in, so I might smell her there..."

# Kidnapping

*Do good and cast it into the sea* —Arabic proverb.

The old women in my hometown used to say, "Do good and cast it into the sea". I would hear this without knowing what it meant, until one frightening day, when I not only understood the proverb but lived its meaning for real, and not in theory.

I did not wait for appreciation or a salary in exchange for my humanitarian work with aid groups and relief organizations that worked in the Syrian towns and cities hit by the most violent shelling and destruction, nor did I wait for acknowledgement of my work in the vast camps near the border. I did not wait for thanks from anyone but God. For me, the greatest reward was when I can put a smile on a child's face after offering them something they loved, or when I hear a prayer straight from the heart of an old woman who would lift her hands to the sky and say:

'May God preserve your youth for your mother and family.'

But I did not expect that my life could be a gift from someone I didn't know, and all because of a simple good deed that I had done and forgotten. This was what happened with me on that frightening day.

\* \* \*

I do not remember the features of the masked person who gazed at me with eyes flooding with gratitude. It's hard to remember someone from their eyes if you have not seen their other features.

*Kidnapping*

He was standing a few meters away from the border gate that allows people to cross into Turkey. These people are normally sick, injured, disabled, or workers with humanitarian and relief organizations, of which I was one.

I was waiting for my name to be called. It was written on a paper, sitting in the hands of a Turkish officer who was responsible for allowing us to enter. Before my turn, a woman in distress arrived, holding a child whose head was resting on her shoulder and whose legs were stretched out in a line down to her knees. She tried to convince the officer at the gate to let her enter. I understood from what she was saying that the child needed to be urgently taken by an ambulance to a Turkish hospital. But the officer, who didn't speak Arabic except for a few words necessary to his job—and mostly two words that he repeated all day, allowed and forbidden—did not understand her. All he could see was that she wanted to enter even though her name was not written on the list, so he was repeatedly and impatiently saying, *"Mamnoe"'* to mean forbidden. He struggled to pronounce the last letter of the word, since its vowel does not exist in the Turkish language.

He would forget himself and start to shout in both Arabic and Turkish, "Yasak, yasaaaak. Mamnoe, Mamnoeeee".

There were many who wanted to pass through the crossing for urgent medical reasons. The Turkish soldiers weren't heartless stone, but they were merely following strict orders. Many times, I saw their tears as they rushed to help the injured into an ambulance while praying that God would help them avenge themselves on their oppressors.

The distressed mother tried again to explain her child's case, but in vain. Meanwhile, the masked man was listening carefully to their discussion.

*Kidnapping*

I understood that the child suffered from renal failure and needed dialysis, and that, if they waited until the next day, he would die. The hospital that had been regularly helping the child in Syria had been targeted and taken out of service. I tried to intervene, but the Turkish officer seemed to be programmed like a machine, repeating "forbidden" incessantly.

He started to explain this to me, so that I could explain it to the woman, since he knew my face, as I'd passed in and out through the humanitarian crossing many times. From him, I understood that only fifty people could enter a day, and only those who came at the beginning of the day. Then he started to shake the list of names and repeat again and again, "forbidden."

"Only those on this list enter. The injured and sick come in the morning, and that's that."

I saw the child's mother was in distress, and that the father had sent his wife to talk to the officer, perhaps thinking the officer would feel kinder toward her as a mother. This inspired me with an idea.

"My name's on the list," I told him. "Since the number is limited, I'd like to give my name to this woman, so she can enter instead of me."

The people around us who spoke Turkish pushed the case, explaining the child's situation and telling the officer that he was in a state of crisis. In the end, the officer agreed to let the woman enter instead of me. He deleted my name from the list and asked the woman about the child's name. I remember she said "Omar," but I do not remember his surname.

Then there was a new problem: her husband. It was clear the woman was simple-minded, and would not manage the situation without him, so the

*Kidnapping*

father had to accompany his child. But the officer refused, so we tried to convince him. I knew officers like him did not like to argue, and if they said *yok*, which means no in Turkish, then it was not negotiable. Still, I did not lose hope of trying to spark feelings of mercy towards the child. Again, I started to explain the child's situation, which was very dangerous, and told him that the mother alone would not be able to cope with the obstacles or figure out where to go and how.

Then he said: "You work with doctors, so you can help her".

"If there were a hospital or electricity," I said, "no one would have come here. She will enter instead of me, and it's important that the father enters with the child". Then the officer gradually started to ease up, explaining to me that he was only an officer following orders, and he could not bypass the rules and the system, and if he did so, repercussions would await him.

Eagerly, I told him, "God will not let you come to harm so long as you are doing good for Him, and nothing is lost to God, not even an atom". I continued preaching about goodness because I felt he was religious, since he used religious words more than once—such as the name of God and the Prophet Muhammed—and also he had said in Arabic "There's no strength nor power except in God". I kept insisting.

"Do good and cast it in the sea," I said.

He liked the proverb and said that his grandfather has once told something like that, and he wanted to know the meaning of it, so I explained that it was a traditional Arab proverb. He liked it a lot and started to repeat the words, as if he were trying to memorize it.

*Kidnapping*

"Do good and cast it in the sea," he uttered with difficulty.

I was happy, as was the woman, when the officer decided that the father could be allowed to enter with his wife and child. He seemed affected by the proverb, and maybe he thought it was a verse from the Quran or one of the sayings of the Prophet.

When the officer gave his consent, the woman called to her husband, who has been patiently waiting through my argument. The husband hurriedly removed his mask and got the child from his wife, then went ahead to the internal gate. I couldn't remember his features, but I remember his rough voice from when he thanked me and insisted on knowing my name. The mother also prayed for me warmly, her heart seared by pain from her child's predicament.

I turned back, having lost my turn, and told the officer: "Do good and cast it in the sea".

He repeated the phrase with his flimsy Turkish accent and smiled.

As I left, I felt relief well up inside me. I felt the pleasure of helping that family, although at the same time I was thinking about how to enter, now that I'd relinquished my turn.

Days passed, and I forgot the story, since many things happen every day.

Weeks later, I heard that a man named Abu Omar entered from Turkey with his wife and child, and that they came searching for me in the border area but didn't find me. I heard from my colleagues that he wanted to thank me for the good turn I have done for his family. But I didn't mention that goodness until the frightening day came.

*Kidnapping*

On that frightening day, I was bent over, trying to pick up bags of fruit I had bought, when an iron fist yanked me from behind and I was dragged into a car. The car's door closed, and then the brakes gave a snarling sound, and the vehicle that looked like a wolf that had just captured its prey, moved off with the speed of lightning. All of that happened in the blink of an eye.

I was with my older brother, who was imprisoned in one of the regime's detention centers, and passed horrible moments until he was, by some miracle, released. He often joined me in my travels, especially my stories about the kidnappings by unknown parties were on the rise. My brother had visited me in the morning and suggested taking a vacation in our hometown with the family, and he convinced me by mentioning how much my mother wanted to have this family reunion, and to see us all together sitting at one table, as we had not been for years.

I sat beside him in his car as we headed to Idlib's Maaret al-Numan city. By evening, we were on the Saraqib Bridge, where a vendor was putting out boxes of fruits, waiting to sell it to people passing by in their cars. I asked my brother to stop and buy some fruits, and he agreed right away.

"You go ahead while I go to a gas station near here and fill the car," he said.

It was only a few minutes before I'd put the bags at the edge of the street while the vendor, who was a few meters away, started reorganizing his goods. That's when a hand grabbed me and a car swallowed me and moved off like an arrow, leaving the fruit that dropped from my hands and rolled onto the street.

*Kidnapping*

Suddenly, I found myself in a darkened sedan, and one of them grabbed my t-shirt and pulled it over my head while another held my arm and yanked it wildly backward and handcuffed me. A hand reached out and patted me down from the top of my head to my toes and found nothing except my wallet containing my ID and some money. During the first seconds, I did not realize what had happened. I felt like I was chocking and was not able to scream, my heart thudding against my chest so fiercely as if it might fly out of my trembling body. My ears were filled with the loud buzzing that was circulating in my head. It was a matter of seconds, and then I realized I had been kidnapped. When the car passed a bump in the road, I felt it fly in the air then crash to the ground. Those inside the car hit its roof, and since I was handcuffed, I almost fell off the seat. One shouted at the driver saying,

"Slow down! You could've killed us. We're far away now."

The car then started to slow down. At the same time, I heard voices around me saying, "Are you sure he was the one we want? Maybe we made a mistake. He doesn't seem like the right one."

Another man said in a high, squeaky voice, "I'm sure he's the one. I saw him more than once at the border in the camps. And the *sheikh* said he's blond with blue eyes and is carrying a backpack. I followed him from the border to Saraqib Bridge".

The first one disagreed. "Man, this is an Arab, not a foreigner. Take a look at his civil ID. His name is Hasan."

I was trying to gather my strength to scream in their faces: "What do you want from me?", but their argument was louder than my voice that disappeared inside the cave of my mouth.

No doubt they thought I was a foreigner because of my clothes or blond hair, so they kidnapped me to trade in for a big ransom. That was what one of them said.

"He seems like a foreigner with a Syrian ID. Maybe his ID is fake. Anyway, this one could bring us a lot of cash."

I knew that my features, and the way I dressed, made a lot of people think I was not from the area. Many would see me with the teams of foreigners, and so they would infer I was one of them. Maybe this was the reason I have been kidnapped three times, although every time there was a different story. Once, I almost lost my head.

However, their accents were not foreign to me, and they sounded very close to our local accent. They had to be from the region, so I suddenly shouted, "Who are you? What do you want from me?"

The man with the high-pitched voice answered. "We don't want anything from you, but you're welcome to stay with us for a few days, and then we'll sell you to your family."

The words *sell you to your family* hit my brain, and I pictured my mom when she would hear about my kidnapping.

I remembered my brother who had gone to fill up the car. He must have gotten back and discovered I was not waiting him on the bridge. He would ask the fruit vendor, but had the vendor seen the car that kidnapped me?

Maybe yes. Maybe no. Everything had happened in a flash, and even I did not notice the car that was behind me while I was putting the bags down on the street. But my brother must have seen the fruit spilled out onto the street.

*Kidnapping*

He would know that something had happened to me—that someone with a car had kidnapped me—but what would he tell my mom and my family?

I felt the car leaving the main street. It turned to the right and seemed as though it had entered a road full of potholes. The car zigzagged from right to left and my head smacked against the glass more than once. The driver slowed down and one of them asked me, "What does your father do?"

I didn't answer, but instead I shouted: "Who are you? Are you revolutionaries or thieves?"

A new rude voice chortled and said, "We're thieves".

Then the person who asked me about my father repeated his question: "What does your father do?"

"Nothing" I said.

"How does he do nothing?"

"He was working in real estate."

The person with the squeaky voice said, "Real estate means buying and selling, which means your father is rich. Sweet. Now you have to talk to him and tell him to bring us 100,000."

Then he asked, "Is 100,000 good? Or should we make it 200,000? It seems you're pampered and dear to your mom."

These thugs who kidnapped me did not care about who I was or what I did. Their only interest was to get the ransom.

I started imagining how they would torture me to force my family to pay up. I thought of asking them about their big boss, so I could try to make a deal with him. But from the way they were talking, I could not figure out who among them was the most important person or their leader. All of them spoke at the same time, and all of them talked over each other. I could not figure out who was giving orders to the others. I asked them to take off the handcuffs because they were cutting into my wrists, but they did not listen.

"You always go through the border crossing," one of them said. "Do you work with journalists or organizations?"

"Why did you kidnap me?" I asked. "I swear I am with nobody and my work is all with humanitarian organizations."

"Humanitarian organizations for who? For the regime? And are you also working with journalists?"

"Humanitarian organizations?" another one said. "By God, you're all thieves. You steal aid and sell it."

Another one said: "Not only do they sell the aid, but they also get their salaries in dollars."

A third one threatened me. "I swear you'll pay us everything you get in dollars. I swear that you're the thieves of the revolution. You stole the people's blood."

I couldn't bear what he was saying. His words were like whips to my ears, so I screamed as loud as I could: "We're the youth of the revolution, and the men, and you're its thieves who kidnap people in exchange for ransom. For three years I've been working as a volunteer without any money, not in dollars or Syrian pounds. I help people and the needy, whether they're suffering from cold, rain, snow, or shelling."

I expected them to hit me for cursing them, but I was surprised to hear a man who I thought was speaking for the first time. "If you're like you say you are, then we'll know when we get there and check with the sheikh, but if you're lying, there's going to be hell to pay."

Then he changed his tone, addressing the others: "I don't think he's the guy we want."

"The *sheikh* described him like this."

"Anyway, we're almost there," another one said.

My t-shirt, which they had wrapped around my head to cover my eyes, was transparent, so I saw the large home the car drove up to. They got out, leaving me handcuffed, and closed the doors behind them. Their footsteps faded until the place was quiet, and I felt like a carcass thrown in an abandoned cemetery.

In the frightening darkness, horrible demons pounded in my chest as I imagined the ways in which they would torture me in order to blackmail my family into paying ransom.

I imagined many strange and terrible things, as I heard a lot about kidnaping cases. I imagined that they would hang me by a rope in an abandoned well, and then would close the opening with a rock, and that they would throw a loaf of bread to me, and the rats would fight me for the bread. After that, they would drop me a mobile phone to call my family, especially my mom, to ask her to sell all their property in order to pay the ransom. I also imagined they would agree on a place to leave the money and then would ask my family to leave, and that they would get the money and forget me in the well to die of hunger or from being eaten by wild rats.

I began asking God to help me, and said all the prayers I have memorized, asking Him to rescue me from this catastrophe. I reminisced of what they had said in the car and tried to identify them—whether they were bandits, thieves or revolutionaries—and whether they were looking for someone else and had confused him with me. They said they would bring me in front of the *sheikh*. So, who is this *sheikh*? Was he the leader of a gang or a revolutionary military faction? I felt cold tremors run all through my spine, and I wondered if they were loyal to the regime and would bring me in to be arrested. Death would be more merciful, since I have heard about what detainees faced in the regime's dark cells.

I tried to arrange my thoughts. How would I confront him? What should I say, at the start? Before I could come up with a plan for a speech among my many contending thoughts, I heard an iron door open violently and heavy footsteps strike the ground. They hit my chest as well. Then an angry man with a rough voice asked: "Where is he? May God destroy your homes!"

Before I heard a reply, the sedan door opened with a creak like the angel Israfil's trumpet, and a bright light was focused on my body, which was crammed onto the seat.

"Here he is," someone said, and the man with the rough voice said, "Show me his face!"

The bright light poured into my eyes, and I could not see anybody, but I heard the rough voice curse harshly, "You cows, you donkeys, you son of...."

*Kidnapping*

Then rushing toward me, yanking off my handcuffs, and speaking in the same tone,

"Mr. Hasan? Oh, you animals! This is Mr. Hasan... Come here! Come here, Hasan."

And he hugged me.

I could not understand what was happening as he took my hand and walked with me through the darkness in the courtyard. I was no able to comprehend what he was saying. When we entered a room, I saw his face ... I focused on his eyes, and they were familiar to me, but they were full of apologies.

When a man said "Uncle Abu Omar," I remembered the eyes of the man who was watching me, waiting, while I was arguing with a Turkish officer at the border crossing.

He hugged me again. "I'm so ashamed, son of my brother". Then he turned toward the other men. "I sent you to arrest a military spy and informant at the border and you brought me the man who saved the life of my son Omar."

He hugged me and said with a shaky voice, "For God's sake, forgive me, my son". When he left, after hugging me, I saw two heavy tears crawling from his eyes into his scraggly beard. Shocked at this sight, I did not know what to say.

I imagined the face of the Turkish officer, saying the Arabic proverb in his Turkish accent: "Do good and cast it into the sea".

*Kidnapping*

I heaved a deep sigh. "Thanks to God. Do good and cast it into the sea"

\* \* \*

I wrote in my notebook:

The kidnapping chapter is not a personal one, but rather one of the darkest chapters in the stories of wars in general, and the Syrian war in particular. Many gangs were formed to exploit the chaos and the absence of the rule of law. Most of these gangs started up on the regime side from the first days of demonstrations, when the regime released its mercenary *shabbiha* to wreak havoc on the people and suppress the demonstrations. Time passed, and they formed organized gangs to kidnap people. They frightened thousands and gathered millions of pounds and dollars in exchange for the life of the detainees. This was the trade of war, the trade of souls.

There were traders who made a business from people's lives, hiding behind the names of flashy humanitarian organizations as they begged on behalf of those who lived in the open, and made a business from trading in the blankets people used to protect themselves from the heat of summer or the cold of winter.

I have met many of these people who wear fake humanitarian masks, or even religious ones--those who grew their beards long for religious reasons while their wallets were full of dollars and riyals. They exploited the situation in the camps to gratify their personal desires. Some of them searched the camps for underage women alone and in need, and they would marry them under the pretext of helping them according to the Quran and the

*Kidnapping*

Prophet's teachings. These child marriages among the minors in the camps escalated as a result of misery and deprivation.

I remember that, once, I offered a toy to a thirteen-year-old boy and another to his sister, who was a year younger. When I met the child again, after a year, he remembered me and said sadly, "Do you want my sister's toy? She left it in the house".

I did not dare ask him where his sister had gone, afraid that he would say she had died, but he said, "She got married".

I was furious and headed towards her mother's tent. When I asked her why she had done this, she smiled coldly and said, "Marriage protects girls".

"But she's a little child," I said.

"Her other three sisters got married before her, and at the same age."

Then she began babbling her illogical words of justification, not even a syllable of which I found convincing. I have heard similar speeches about poverty and being in need and babies born out of wedlock so many times. After a year, I met the boy again, and he told me that he wanted two toys for his sister's daughters, since she has given birth to twins and that then her husband left back to his country.

This was not only limited to individuals—states also carried out such cruel actions in the names of Syrian refugees. These were states that claimed to be Islamic and Arab, and some of these countries closed their doors in the faces of immigrants escaping death. At the same time, some European countries opened their doors and communities to them.

*Kidnapping*

\* \* \*

This war is cursed. Some people work day and night without waiting for a reward, only for the sake of God and for humanitarian reasons, regardless of the obstacles, insults, and the risks that can include death. But on the other side, others are keen to exploit the war as business to earn millions and make it a market to buy slaves for their desires.

# Suns drowning in the mud

**I wrote in my notebook:**

**W**hen you see them from afar, you would think these were blue flags surrendering to the blue sky in the face of fate. When you come closer, you see tents scattered across your line of sight, reeling from the blows of the wind. When you enter them, you realize that they are arms pulsing painfully, trying to surround the injured within their small warmth.

These arms draw together those who lived monotonous lives, working the whole day to come back to their homes so they might spend their lives building them— *but the war destroyed, in a moment, what they have built in years.*

They did not find another place to save the lives of their children except for these blue flags, surrendering to the injustice of fate.

\* \* \*

It was a night of treachery for their lives and their safety. Even the day before that night did not offer a clear sky to smile on them from behind a veil of white clouds.

Before the evening of that October day, a medical facility asked us to bring medicine urgently to a martyr's daughter named Amal. Her leg had recently been amputated in a nearby camp on the side of the mountain.

We had to drive seven kilometers along a dirt path rutted by the wheels of cars that had passed through that summer. The road would begin straight,

*Suns drowning in the mud*

then head up towards the terraces that were placed one above the other, gradually going up to the peak of the mountain along the border. Many tents were located there, and within them thousands of stray lives.

When we set out, the sky did not seem as though it was hiding a horrible night. There were light clouds, but little by little, black masses started gathering from the southern and western sides. These masses resembled huge, dark, mythical beasts, as if they had appeared from the depths of history to ride to the top of the sky, with only their sun-colored heads escaping. The scene would seem like tongues of flame chasing the remains of the day.

"Do you see what I see?", I asked my friends.

"There's no doubt it's a big storm," one said.

"It's like night is going to attack us from the heart of the sky," another said.

*God save us*, I said to myself. *May He have mercy on those displaced who are in the open without cover or a roof above their heads.*

The olive, fig, and cypress trees that were planted along the roadsides seemed as though they felt the coming risk, and they looked as though they were starting to panic, as though they would escape and leave their old trunks if they could.

We tried to double our speed so that we would reach our destination before this storm arrives, which was attacking the sky with horrible madness. The storm seemed as though it were sending its breath on ahead as ferocious winds.

*Everything screws/works against those who live in tents, I said to myself. Even the sky.* How are they going to escape from the anger crawling towards them? *It's their fate and that of olive trees alike to face those winds. But there is a significant difference between the olive trees' trunks and those tent pegs. The tents will collapse at the wind's first gust. Whereas olive trees can withstand its howling attacks, its roots clutching the earth below.*

The storm got ahead of us to the camp's gate. People at the camp were in continuous movement as they felt the danger coming from the south. All of them were on alert and in horror. Women were running here and there as the wind played with their long clothes. It almost sent them flying as they gathered their children between the tents. Men were shouting as they checked the tent pegs and put heavy soil and stones on the sides of the tents. Elderly people stopped at the doors, shouting at others to enter, as the darkness began to cover the blueness of the camp. Some lights here and there scattered and stovepipes sent up their smoke, as though elves were playing in the face of the cold winds that sang and whistled along the tents' ropes.

The sky was in league with us—as soon as we entered the desired tent, the rain showers poured violently on the protective roofs.

The girl with the amputated leg was lying in her bed. Her mother welcomed us with gratitude and prayers, telling us she would never be able to properly reward us. While the girl covered herself up to her neck, her eyes overflowed with a melange of gratitude and pain. The bodies of the girl's three brothers were crammed in beside her, and they extended their small heads, pushing out with their shoulders to look at us. I almost heard their teeth chattering from the cold.

*Suns drowning in the mud*

The sound of the rain slamming wildly on the tent's roof overpowered the mother's voice as she asked us to rest a bit. At the insistent sound of the rain and the mother, who implored that we rest a little, we found ourselves unable to leave.

I asked her about the girl and her health, and she told us her story in a loud voice, as though shouting:

"Amal, my poor girl, was in school. I told her thousands of times to abandon the school, since it wasn't safe for her any longer, as death was everywhere. But she said to me: my future, it's my future..."

What future? Is there still a country where we can have a future? Life left me this daughter and her brothers after my husband died, but her soul is attached to school. She was studying for her baccalaureate and was amongst the top of her class. She said to me: 'Even if I die, I must go...'

I remembered how a child who stood by the school's door and dreamt of being an architect or engineer, so he could build his homeland. He had refused to be a soldier destroying his country. While he dreamt, a bomb startled him and he died, and the dream remained hidden in his school bag."

Then she addressed me, as though she could see from my eyes that I have been affected by her tears: "My son, death is easy, but being disabled is harder than death".

I asked her: "What happened next?"

"In the morning, at 8 a.m., the time the girls entered the school, a warplane came flying in and bombed the school door. God had mercy, as most of them had already entered and were inside. Had it been seconds

*Suns drowning in the mud*

earlier, there would have been a massacre. More than 100 girls were near the door. It was an act of God that some were saved. Four rockets were fired, hitting the door and leaving a 10-meter hole. All the shops and stands on the street were broken, and part of the fence collapsed. Half of Amal's body was under the collapsed fence while the other half begged for them to pull her from Death's maw. One leg stayed under the rubble while the other thigh was smashed like dough."

Lightning flashed and lit up the pale darkness to that its glare snatched away our sight. I heard the woman saying:

"There is no god but God, may God save us from this night."

I saw tears in the girl's eyes and her weak voice whispered, asking her mom to bring her cousin who could give her an injection of painkillers. The sky replied to her with horrible thunder, booming as though it had thrown mountains of rocks rolling over the camps. The children shouted in one faltering voice and bent over their sister, screaming:

"Oh, God, my leg hurts."

The mother rushed to push the children away from her, but she said:

"Do not be afraid, Mama. Don't be afraid!"

One of the frightened children said in horror: "Mama, have the jets come?"

"No, darling," the mother said. "The thunder is the rain's voice. This is mercy from God."

*Suns drowning in the mud*

The child then rolled himself, like a cat, into his mother's lap and buried his head in her warm chest as the sky opened rivers of rain on wings of powerful winds that madly struck at the tent.

The tent swayed as though it had been hit by a tornado.

"Did you check the tent from the outside, auntie?" I asked.

She nodded.

"Some good people fixed it. Since afternoon, people in the area have been saying they saw clouds coming in from the south and that a storm would come so to take precautions."

Along with the sound of the rain and the wind, people's voices rose outside, and there were recitations of Quranic verses, shouting, screaming, crying with supplications.

"Give me the shovel!"

"Oh, good people help us! Water is drowning the tent."

"Hold the rope, son, and stretch it so I can hammer in the peg."

"Oh God, you have the solution!"

"Dig around the tent!"

"Clear a ditch for the water!"

Despite the strong winds, we opened the door to the tent. The whole camp—its ground, sky, people, and tents—was full of movement, horror, and shouting. There were floods rushing downhill from high cliffs and the surrounding valleys. Ghosts of people flitted around the tents with battery-supply lights, and the whole place was like a beehive.

Everyone was working, and whenever someone finished fixing a peg or stretching a barrier, they moved to the nearest person who was asking for help. We found ourselves automatically amongst the rushing people, doing what they were doing, from pounding in tent pegs to changing the direction of the flowing water.

From one of the nearby tents, we heard a voice in distress. The tent had almost collapsed in the floodwaters that were hitting it furiously, about to drag it from the ground. Inside the tent there lay a man who could not move. I saw his leg fixed in a white gypsum cast from above his pelvis down to his toes. The water leaking inside the tent had begun to surround him, but he was paralyzed by the cast. At that moment, I imagined him as my brother, who had spent months in a similar position after his injury in the demonstration. My friends and I started to move the floodwaters away from him while people outside the tent tried to change the water's direction away while re-affixing the pegs, which were about to be pulled out.

An old man who was working beside me said:

"I have never seen rain like this in seventy years."

Another one replied, while digging furiously into the ground with his shovel and holding a lamp between his teeth, such that the light showed his long beard:

"This is God's anger, God's anger."

Someone else in the darkness replied angrily.

*Suns drowning in the mud*

"Oh, my sheikh! What anger is this? Fear God and don't say such things about children who are drowning in the mud."

Before the dialogue turned into an argument, a woman opened a tent's flap and the light poured inside as she called for help.

"Oh, good people! A woman is going to die! Help us!"

Without knowing what I was doing, I headed toward the source of voice, and I found an elderly woman blocking the entrance of the tent with her full height. When she saw me, she said, "My son, God help you, we need a car".

"What happened, auntie?" I asked.

"My son's wife is in terror and she is about to give birth."

I did not know how to answer. I imagined a family drowning in water or set on fire, but I had not imagined a woman would go into labor at such a moment.

The elderly woman continued talking to a woman who walked nearby.

"The woman is seven months pregnant, and perhaps it isn't the right time to give birth, but because she's frightened, it will happen. We want to help her before she and her baby end up dying."

Other women rushed toward the tent, and one of them said:

"Your son's wife is only in her eighth month, like my daughter, and she's not ready to give birth."

"Sister, it's because she's frightened," the old woman said.

*Suns drowning in the mud*

As I thought about bringing a car, I remembered that it was impossible for a car to get up that muddy way that went down to the medical station. I turned and waited to see what was going to happen, and at the same time I heard a baby scream, as though challenging the storm with the power of life.

Once, a doctor who works in a hospital told me that the percentage of births in camps was high for a variety of reasons. One reason is people's desire to compensate for the lives lost in the war. Sometimes it was the desire to pull their name from the mouth of Death. These people fought death in their own ways. That day, the doctor had laughed and said: "And perhaps because there's a lack of work."

The storm lasted for more than an hour, and then it began to calm down in fits and starts, as though recovering its breath, and then changing again, pounding on the tents with even greater force.

The water dripped from my head to my toes, and I could no longer feel my numbed feet, as my shoes were full of water and heavy with mud. I started searching for my friends while people began to calm down. I found my friends gathered in the car, trying to turn on the heater that was not working. We tried to wring out our clothes to dry them as much as possible, but the weather was cold, so we considered making an adventure of going back to the camp as not to die of the cold.

The car's light might have drawn people's attention to us after the storm started to weaken. Suddenly, an elegant man wrapped in a coat knocked on the car's glass. He invited us to his tent and we did not wait until he insisted to accept his invitation. He took us to his tent and apologized on behalf of the

*Suns drowning in the mud*

people who were preoccupied with their misfortunes and had not taken the time for us.

As soon as we entered his tent, we felt a caring warmth, quite delighted to see he had a working kerosene stove. We almost hugged the stove, our bodies quivering from the freezing frost bite. I felt a numbness running from my finger through my toes. We got rid of our outer clothes and hung them up to dry. Then I started navigating the tent, as, in the beginning, I had not noticed its strange contents.

There was a dirty worn-out blackboard hung in the middle of the place, and childish drawings of fruits, jets, and tanks festooned the board. There was a plastic can full of different kinds of used pens. I saw, in one corner, piles of books and notebooks. I asked our host's permission and then picked up a notebook in which flowers, children, jets, and cannons had been drawn. I also saw toys made with a great deal of imagination from sardine cans and other junk. Before I said anything to our host, he already knew what I wanted to ask.

"I'm a teacher. My name is Abdullatif."

I asked, surprised, "Is this a school?"

"Almost!" he said, then gave me a sad laugh. "We do our duty with what comes to hand."

We discovered that our host was an old teacher who had been working in the high schools of Damascus. After showing his solidarity with the revolution, he started to feel the risk of being arrested. One day, before his house was surrounded to be searched by security forces, he fled toward the liberated areas and, from there, he continued to the border areas, and was about to enter Turkey but changed his mind at the last moment.

*"Happiness is not confined to a certain place,"* he said, *"but is instead a decision.* I made my decision to be happy here, where I draw a smile over the saddened hearts of children at this camp."

After that, he kept silent for a while, and then went on.

"When I arrived at this camp, I found I could be in direct contact with the massive scale of this tragedy and its wounds. The wounds that captured me are the homeland's wounds. They opened my eyes to many facts. One fact is that I believe it is mere treachery to leave the homeland to enjoy life, safety, peace, and what people imagined is happiness in Europe.

As I lived with deprived children, who were barefoot and naked, I found it shameful to leave them after they have already been left by their fathers, who were killed or already deceased. It's treachery to leave here with my knowledge, abandoning children to illiteracy, after schools have been destroyed. I had no choice but to transform my tent into a school so that the children of the camps could gather here and I could teach and play with them all day long. They remind me of the grandchildren I left in the regime-controlled areas. Thus far, I have not managed to find a way to get them out of Damascus.

I feel the warmth of the children of the camp as they would come in the morning, first gathering around the kerosene stove, as most tents did not have stoves inside. Some tents had firewood stoves, but the problem is that the wood was wet and would not burn. Or, if it did burn, it would make a lot of smoke that would suffocate the people who lived all around. So, children escaped from war to live in this indescribable situation: either they would die frozen from the cold or burned or suffocated by smoke.

While the teacher was speaking, I recalled a memory of a burned child whom we pulled from a charred pile inside a tent that had burned completely before someone could reach him. "Yes," I said. "Last winter I saw a child die in a fire."

"Was it in Qah camp?" he asked me.

"Yes."

"I heard about it, but I didn't know how it happened. I would like you to tell me about it because I'm interested in gathering the details of such a tragedy."

I spoke about that painful day:

"They told us that he was his parents' sole child. His parents were constantly quarreling. Every night, the child would hear them fighting, exchanging curses and beatings. They said the husband was threatening his wife, saying that he would marry again, while the wife accused him of torturing her by hanging out with one of the girls in the camp.

On the night of the incident, they said the fight between the couple was intense, and the husband had been heard swearing that he'd divorce his wife and force her out of the tent. Their neighbor told me that she tried to ease the fight before things got all the way to a divorce, and the miserable child was witnessing their fight, and his crying was heard all night.

*Suns drowning in the mud*

"The neighbor also said: 'When the father threw the mother outside, the child grabbed onto her and tried to leave with her, barefoot in mud that might drown him.

"But I stopped him and said that I would bring her back, and meanwhile I didn't know where his father had gone. I told the boy to put on his new boots and that I would be back soon. The boy said that the boots were full of water and his mom didn't allow him to dry them on the stove. I went away and, before I reached his mother beside the camp gate, the tent was on fire. He must have tried to dry his boots on the stove, and the fire burned his clothes and then the canvas tent as well."

"Why didn't they ask for help from the firefighters?" the teacher asked me.

"Impossible." I smiled.

"It was impossible because, on that day, I saw the fire burn the tent as quickly as a flash, and then the tent collapsed into smithereens. I saw the divorced mother return amid people's voices. The mother tried more than once to throw herself into the fire to save her child, but people held her. The father was sitting on the pile of ashes, hitting his temples with his fists. His whimpering still breaks my heart till today."

The teacher interrupted me, absent-mindedly.

*"These children are the true victims of this war."*

That moment, Fate seemed to be listening, and it wanted to emphasize what the teacher was saying, as a screaming asked for help:

*Suns drowning in the mud*

"Oh people! Good people, the child died."

We were the first to reach the source of the voice. As a light reflected from an opened door, I could see a woman standing like a statue, frozen with horror, stretching her arms.

In her arms, there was a child wrapped in a blanket with his arms and legs hanging out. She was staring at the child, screaming: "He died! He died!" People gathered around and took the child from her arms and drew her inside.

We returned to the tent trembling in shock.

"I think he died because of the cold," the teacher said.

"Because of cold?" someone asked.

"Yes. The frost here can freeze adults, let alone children. That child was only three months old. I saw him more than once in his mother's lap, as she comes to visit me every morning with her children before all the others arrive, and she would fire up the stove for them. She told me that it was no good firing up her stove because wet firewood was impossible to light, and even if it burned, it would smoke a lot and it would choke them. She also said once that dying of cold was better than suffocating to death on smoke."

He sighed and went on. "The child was as beautiful as the moon. He had no problems or diseases. He must have died because of the cold."

The teacher Abdullatief kept silent, and his features seemed struck by what had happened. I imagined that a tear was hiding deep in those eyes that were surrounded by wrinkles.

*Suns drowning in the mud*

\* \* \*

The next day, we rose to the sound of chirping. It was not birds, but dozens of children under the age of ten. They surrounded the teacher's tent, singing and laughing. It was as though nothing frightening had happened on the previous day. Even the sunny sky seemed to deny how it had wronged these people.

One child opened the door and asked,

"Teacher! Do we have classes today or should we play?"

"I have guests today. Wait for me in the square."

When we left the square, our car got stuck in the mud. The children were behind us, alongside their teacher. Their shabby clothes were of all colors, and their feet were stuck in the mud as they waved to us, their smiles lit not by the cold sun, but by the warmth of their imaginations.

As we drove away, I imagined them as *suns rising from the mud.*

# World Without Names

### Dead Yet Still Alive

It was unbelievable that Osman would appear on TV. Osman—my son?

Um Osman shouted, unconvinced, into the face of the neighbor girl who had told her the news.

"Yes, I swear, auntie," the girl said, confirming the news. "They announced it as breaking news in red, and said that the TV would broadcast an interview with Osman M.R.".

Again, the mother shouted.

"Yes, this is my son's name, but what would bring him to the TV? Why would he appear on TV?"

"I do not know," the girl replied, an intentional avoidance of answering Um Osman's question or giving her a reason. It is worth noting that the mother had not heard from her son for a year and half.

"When will this interview be broadcast, my daughter?" the mother asked.

The girl got out her mobile and searched for the airing time. "My father says it will be showed after the evening news, which means in three hours and a quarter".

The three and a quarter hours were too long for the mother to wait. The minutes were slow, spent in misery, and the seconds were longer than the entirety of her life. It was longer than the thirty-one years she spent waiting for her husband, who was arrested in the 1980s and of whom she had no news so far, except that he was in the Palmyra prison. Some said her husband had died in the massacre that had been committed at this infamous prison, but Um Osman continued waiting. Osman had been a few months old, and his brother Ahmad a year and a few months old. She devoted her life to raising them and getting them an education, until they graduated from university—in her eyes, even then they were still children who needed to be fed. She would wake up at night to check their blankets, fearing a breeze might hurt them.

Ahmad, who earned a law degree, could not find a job due to the security reports against him, which led to a blacklisting, as his father's name was connected to the Muslim Brotherhood—a movement that had revolted against the Syrian regime in the 1980s, especially in Hama.

He had been forced to travel and work as a laborer in Lebanon. He was not able to come back to Syria after the revolution, fearing he would be arrested at the border and sent to the army as backup. Even though he was thirty-two-years-old, this did not matter—the army would take men who were even forty. Osman stayed with his mother and never abandoned her. Even when he was at university, he would come back in the evenings to be with her.

When the revolution started, Um Osman knew her son participated in a demonstration where he recited a poem that inflamed people's enthusiasm. That made her crazy and worried about him, and she wished she could bind him with iron chains so that he would not go out again. She plead with him and cried even more. She would nearly kiss his feet in an effort to get him to promise her that he would not participate in any demonstration again. She got sick and stayed in bed, and no one knew about her secret disease until laboratory analysis revealed that she had an incurable cancer. After that, Ahmad did not participate in demonstrations and stayed with his mom, who always repeated the common saying.

"Oh son, after you burn your mouth on hot milk, you blow on your yogurt

This is originally a Turkish proverb that denotes

(how overcautious a person might become once having experienced something unpleasant)."

"Son, this regime is the oppressor. Assad the father destroyed Hama, Aleppo, and Jisr al-Shoughour."

Sometimes, he would swear to her that they in the demonstrations they only chanted for "freedom and peace," but she would shout in his face, "My darling, what did your father do? I swear he did nothing bad against the state. He spent his time moving between our farmland and home and vice versa. All that happened was that some guests came to our home late at night and had no place to stay. For God's sake, we let them in so they could stay till morning, and then they left. The next day, your father was arrested under the pretext that he hosted members of the Muslim Brotherhood in his house. Your father left and never came back".

Despite giving promises and swearing oaths that he would not go back to demonstrating, Um Osman wanted her son to be more tied to a particular life, so she convinced him to marry his cousin, as they were in love. She had seen him more than once sending her messages and poems, but he was postponing marriage until he could improve his situation, as he said. The

*World Without Names*

mother said to herself that, if her son were in relationship and had children, then he would forget about the demonstrations. "Oh son," she told him. "I'm sick, and I have one request before I die. I want to see your children.".

Osman listened to her. Yet, the doctors told him that she would die, especially as chemotherapy was no longer available in the more liberated areas, as it was very expensive.

He married his cousin Abir. A few days after their marriage, he sold her golden jewelry and got a first dose of chemotherapy for his mom. The second dose was supposed to be after 23 days, but he had nothing except his motorbike, so he headed to the market in Idlib to sell it. He went, and never returned.

And now, the neighbor's girl was telling her, "Osman will be on TV".

Abir came in, holding her baby, and heard Osman's name mentioned in the conversation. So, she asked, "Aunt, what happened? Did I hear Osman's name?"

Happily, his mother said, "Yes! Osman will be on TV. He has always dreamt of reciting his poems on TV".

Then she asked, with a grim look on her face and her eyes cast away from everyone else, "But where was he? For sure he was in Lebanon with his brother. He must have become an important poet, and now he will recite his poems on TV".

She moved her eyes to the cousin her son had loved for many years and spoke in a language mixed with tears and smiles.

"Certainly, he wrote you beautiful poems, and for little Osman," she gestured at the baby, "more beautiful ones".

It felt like an eternity for Osman's mother and wife before the time finally came for the news. The electric generator was ready in case the power went out, as they feared to happen.

The news ended, and they heard that the Syrian Arab Army had hit terrorists' locations across the country, from north to south, from desert to sea. Was the whole homeland a place of terrorists?

Finally, the presenter appeared and said:

"Dear viewers, security forces are always alert, and their eyes never shut, as to maintain the security and safety of their citizens. They have managed to target collaborators who aimed at sending the country's security into chaos and destroying citizens' lives and public property. They searched the terrorists' hiding places and arrested the group's leader and its foreign fighters. Weapons made in Israel and US-made night-vision binoculars were confiscated."

After that, the camera showed piles of rifles, machine guns, and bombs.

The mother turned toward her daughter-in-law and asked:

"Haven't they finished with this news? May their tongues be cut out! We've heard enough of their lies."

As if he had heard her, the presenter continued. "Ladies and gentlemen, now we will meet a terrorist group leader, and the one who carried out the attack on the national security building in Idlib's al-Maara district, assassinating innocent men who were defending their homeland. The criminal terrorist Osman MR..."

The camera turned to show a face smudged with makeup that failed to hide the blue bruises around his bulging eyes, set in a skull-like face.

The mother shouted: "Oh, my son, Osman my son.... Lies, lies, lies!"

* * *

I met Um Osman for the first time in 2012, when we were distributing humanitarian aid in the area around the Serjilla caves. That was before the interview with her son aired on TV.

Serjilla is an important ancient region in the Zawiya Mountain, and its history goes back to the first century CE. It was abandoned some 2000 years ago, in the middle of the third century, as a result of natural disasters and a plague-like epidemic. It witnessed social and economic prosperity in the fourth century and then, in the tenth, it was abandoned again. In 2011, people who were escaping the shelling in nearby villages and towns found shelter in its caves and bathhouses, which shielded them from warplanes, or so they thought.

That day, I asked myself: "Did the war send Syria a thousand years back in time so that people would seek shelter from the regime's jets in the Serjilla caves? This was happening at the same time as other nations were thinking of extending their reach to outer space and settling on other planets".

In one of Serjilla's homes that had been abandoned for a thousand years, I met Um Osman. Even though the regime did not care about such important monuments, the houses' structures had been preserved. They were two-story buildings with supporting pillars in the corridors. The upper level was occupied in living and sleeping rooms, while the bottom was used as a storage area for food, supplies, and tools. However, people now used the bottom levels to protect themselves, as the upper ones were without roofs and thus open to jets. Some people stayed in animals' stables or in graves that had black stone coffins carved from huge rocks.

Most of the people of Zawiyah Mountain escaped to the ancient places that surrounded their towns, generally at night, to avoid the barrel bombs thrown during their sleep. Some would return to their hometowns during the day to work in their farms and earn a living.

Um Osman had escaped to these ancient places with her daughter-in-law and grandson, who had not yet been named, waiting until his father came back. They called him "Abu Osman".

When Um Osman knew that we work with humanitarian organizations, she left the corner where she had been sitting, her body thin inside a pitch-black dress, and headed towards us, her back bent so that her hands almost touched the ground. She would extend her head toward me like an elderly turtle with poor eyesight. Symptoms of her illness had appeared all over her body, leaving her pale face carved by the wounds of age and misery.

"Oh son, I have no wish for aid, thanks to God who gives us enough food and water, but I would like you to help me find my son."

I sat next to her, and she began telling me her tear-stained story. I remember some of what she said:

"Osman went to Idlib to sell his motorbike and buy my cancer medication. I did not want him to go because God, all thanks to Him, gave me the strength and will to endure and be patient. He's been gone for a year and four days, and there has been no news about him yet."

When I turned to Abir, wondering about this story, she nodded her head in acquiescence.

"Everyone lies to me—they told me that he'd escaped to Lebanon to visit his brother, and they also said that he went to work in Damascus so that he could afford the price of the medicine. Yet Osman is a good son, and it isn't likely he would go away without telling me. They said there was no way to communicate and that the roads were out of service. But even a mountain wouldn't keep Osman away from his mother. They're all liars—my heart says they arrested him and took him, just like his father, because he'd joined in the demonstrations. Half of the young people were taken and arrested. My heart aches for their stolen youth."

Her moans intensified. "The last time they lied to us was when they took us to the border near Hama to talk to him by phone. They took money for the call—I do not know how much, Abir knows—but everything we were told was lies, lies."

She turned toward Abir. "Let Abir tell you." She pointed out at her daughter-in-law, who was sitting like an antique statue in that abandoned place, while holding her baby. "Tell him, Abir!"

But Abir kept silent, and I discovered that she did not want to talk in front of her mother-in-law.

Hours later, Abir told me secrets Osman's mother did not know, and should not know.

She looked for me when we were distributing aid so as to give me those details she did not want her mother-in-law to hear.

She said: "Osman is neither in Lebanon nor in Damascus. He's being held in Saydnaya Prison, but we did not tell anyone. I swear to you that my mother-in-law would die if she knew. A while ago, a man came and visited us, and he said he'd been detained with my husband in the same prison, and Osman had told him to let us know that they had arrested him from Idlib's main square when he went to sell the motorbike.

The man said that he knows someone who could offer us a phone call with Osman, but that it would cost us 500,000 Syrian pounds. My brother and I sold the land that we'd inherited from our father to get that sum of money. But the man refused to give us an appointment before we gave the money to a third party from Idlib's Maaret al-Numaan district. We did not know the third party, but we were forced to give him the money. The appointment was supposed to be three days after we handed over the money. A month passed, and we—my aunt, little Abu Osman, and I," and here, she nodded at the child, "went to the liberated areas near Hama. Our appointment was at eight in the morning, and we arrived an hour beforehand. I spent two days teaching the child how to say Baba, so that his father, who had never seen him, would hear his voice. I also tickled him so that he would laugh and be heard. I do not know why my aunt made food. She made a lot of the foods that Osman loves," Abir said, while gesturing to the wood stove and black containers nearby. On a high hill near Hama, we sat, waiting in the sun as they told us that's where we'd have coverage for Syriatel service.

144

*World Without Names*

Eight o'clock came, and then it was nine, but no one called. Every time we asked the mediating man, he would tell us to be patient, as perhaps the phone might not have reached Osman, or they could not give it to him at the moment. I do not know why, but my aunt took out the food and said: Come on, people! The food is cold, and Osman has not yet arrived.

When I told her that Osman was not coming, she answered angrily, 'Just let him call, and I will tell him to come, and he will come, because Osman does not refuse my requests. You'll see!'

Then she said again, 'Oh God, the food is cold'.

The mediator said that they might not be able to offer the call that day, but my aunt kept telling him, 'There's no hurry, he will call. Maybe he's in the bathroom. Maybe he's shaving off his long beard, maybe...'.

That day, my aunt seemed to be hallucinating. We waited until afternoon, and no one called. After that, we did not see the man. We did not even know who took the money, and Osman never called."

I promised Abir that I would make every possible effort to search for any detainees freed from Sydnaya prison, so I could bring her news about Osman. I told her that one of my brothers had been arrested, and had been in the same prion, and that I would search for her husband just as I would for my brother.

It was an amazing coincidence that, when my brother was freed from the detention center, he had memorized a lot of the names and addresses of detainees. Human memory was the only thing allowed to capture and smuggle information out of prisons. Most importantly, he had an oral message from a detainee with whom he'd spent time in Sydnaya, for his mother who had cancer. Unfortunately, we have not been able to deliver the message to the mother.

Later, I learned all the stunning details that filled in the gaps in Um Osman's story.

My brother, who had been detained after my other brother was injured, told me:

"I know Osman well from our days in the headquarters of state security.

At night, we'd hear the jingling of keys and then the clanking of the door's lock. Our hearts would drop to the bottom of our ribcage out of fear from the sounds. We'd have to rush to stand so that we were facing the walls. The blood inside our bodies would dry up as we waited for the name the guard would state, and whoever it was would then be driven to an investigation that night. When the name was pronounced, its bearer would head towards the guards without looking at them, extending his hands to be handcuffed, and readying his head for the mask that prevented light from reaching his eyes. Then the prisoner would be pushed through corridors with all kinds of cursing, insults, and punching, and the prisoner wouldn't know where it was coming from. 'Do you want freedom, you son of a bitch? You, you brother of a bitch, do not like Mr. President! Have you, you bastard, forgotten who is your lord and the lord of lords?'

With every word, the iron wires would strike the prisoner, until he arrived in the room with the investigator. The prisoner would be fixed to the ceiling like a ghost, and then slow death would commence.

That day, they opened the door and did not call any name. Instead, they threw a few people inside. One of these people was somehow unconscious.

I'd heard that Osman had been a poet since his schooldays. But, at the time, we weren't friends.

I looked at the face of the unconscious man, bathed in blood oozing from his head, as he was struck by those wires with which they welcomed the detainees.

Dorm 236 was four meters by six, and we were all crammed in that small space that was not large enough for our bodies. We counted tiles that paved the ground, and each person there had less than one tile of space for his body.

The dorm's door clanked, and they threw him in, in a semi-conscious state.

I treated his wounds and tried to calm him, but he kept crying and repeating one sentence:

"'My mom, you guys, my mom has cancer, and I was on my way to buy her chemotherapy treatment, I swear...'

We understood from him that he'd been stopped on the motorbike he meant to sell at a checkpoint in Idlib's main square. They'd yanked off the black scarf he'd wrapped around his head to protect himself from the cold while driving. They made him get off his vehicle, saying he was a terrorist and his scarf was a sign. They dumped the gasoline out of the motorbike and burned it. Then they tied him up and tossed him in their car.

He said he did not know who they were: Were they with the regime? A gang? He did not know.

The next day, when we heard the door's sounds clanking once more, we rushed to the wall. Death awaited those who looked in the faces of the guards. Again, they wanted Osman. They took him, but we forgot to tell him not to confess to anything, and not to tell the 'investigator' about the beating he'd received on the way because if he did, he would be beaten like hell on his way back."

My brother told me that Osman was not lucky: He was accused of murder.

"How?" I asked.

"They'd bring us in front of the investigator, masked and handcuffed. We wouldn't see the investigator. We'd hear only the voice that asked us: Do you confess?

And when you asked him, 'What should I confess to?' they would tie your hands with rope and hang you from the ceiling such that your toes would hardly touch the ground and your arms would be twisted behind your back and lifted above your shoulders. You would hear your ribs crack and then you'd wish for death without being able to reach it. You'd stay like that for hours, and this was called the Ghost method, and it was in this position that you were questioned.

People differed in how much they could tolerate such a method. Some confessed to all the crimes of a lifetime in the first hour, even though in reality they were innocent from the mere crime of even stepping on an ant. Osman was weak, and he confessed to everything. He was a gentle poet and had a lot of feelings, but he could not remain steadfast until the end.

Osman told me about the first session of his investigation:

'They guided me through the door to the room, and then stopped me midway. Through my mask, I could see a ghost-like figure sitting behind a table at the center of the room. The smell of cigarette puffs and rancid alcohol was suffocating. It was a matter of seconds before I was fixed as a ghost between the ceiling and the ground, such that my soul could escape through my shoulders. The investigator replied to the uncontrolled screams I emitted, as I felt my ribs being broken and heard the sound of their cracking, and all the other sounds ringing in my ears.

And they said: 'What happened to you, you bastard? Be a man! Just yesterday, you were holding a gun and killing members of the security forces'.

'I swear to God that I did not do it,' and my swearing irritated him, as though he were God.

Someone behind me hit me with barbed wires. From the first strikes, I felt I was being cleaved in two. I do not know the number of lashes I received because I was numb. Then the person behind me was ordered to stop hitting me, and I was again asked: "Tell me, how did you kill our guys in Idlib's al-Maara district? Do not be stubborn and let me help you".

"I swear, sir, I swear on God the Greatest that I have no piece of information or the faintest idea on the matter."

And before I could complete his sentence, the man shouted in my face: 'Which God and which Greatest? Let him come and save you! Here, no one can save you unless you confess.'

The man was silent for a while as he took a drink, then approached me and spit what was left in his mouth at my masked face. It was a disgustingly smelling wine. After that, I felt a burning ember planted at the bottom of my neck. This was the first cigarette to be extinguished on my body. Then I heard his voice going away, and he said: "Warrant officer! Convince him to confess before I come back!".

'Yes, Sir.'

They stripped off my clothes, including the underclothes and started putting out cigarettes on my body.

The burning whips again started hitting my back, shoulders, head and stomach. In the beginning, I could sense the flagellum sizzling on my skin, but soon I lost conscience. When I opened my eyes, I was back in the dorm with inmates clustered around me, trying to wake me from my coma, some of them massaging my shoulder muscles while others trying to stop the bleeding of my back.

In another interrogation session, they pulled out my fingernails and toenails. In the next session, they threatened me with rape.

All of this, and I did not confess to anything I had not done. But in the end, I confessed to everything they wanted to hear".

Osman wept when I blamed him for confessing to something he had not done. He told me: 'I swear I'm not a coward, I tolerated all kinds of torture: the

Ghost for hours and days; being hit by electric sticks; electric shocks even against my testicles; cigarettes extinguished on every point of my body; my fingernails being pulled out; piss on my head and, several times, in my mouth; and being threatened with rape. I tolerated all of that, but what they threatened me with the night I confessed would've been unbearable for any human".

When I asked him, 'What did they threaten you with?' he cried for a long time and then he stared at my face: "My brother, they repeated the same scenario with me until the investigator went out, asking the torturers to convince me to confess. They beat me until they were tired. They cursed me with the worst words they knew, and that day they made sure I did not lose consciousness. Then voices swarmed around me, and I hung between death and life more than three hours before the door was open, and I heard a voice:

"Osman! Speak! Tell me how they arrested you!"

"Sir, I swear I was going to Idlib to sell my motorbike and get my mother her medicines."

He shouted: "Medicines for your mother?" Then he described my mother with an insulting word I'd never heard before and said, "You're wasting your time and ours, and you do not want us to help you!"

He drank from his glass and spit half its content onto my face and asked again, "Where is your mother, you bastard?"

"In the village."

"Whom does she live with?"

"With me and my wife. We never even leave our home, I swear."

"How old is she?"

"71."

"What about your wife, you bastard?"

"She's 19."

"Is your wife beautiful, you bastard?"

When I did not answer, he went on: "Is her body beautiful? Is sleeping with her sweet?"

I did not answer, so he said, "If you do not want to confess, she will witness our investigation here tomorrow. She will be here naked beside me, and we will be drinking together. Tomorrow, tomorrow. Then he laughed and giggled like a junkie, and he told someone else, "What do you think, officer? Is his 71-year-old mother good for you? I know you're a son of a bitch and you like old women, and you wouldn't let one get away".

"Sir, I await your order."

"What would you think if you went and brought her, and spent with her a happy night?"

I was out of control, and I screamed: "No! My mother, no!"

This time, nobody hit me, but he told me quietly, "Why not? Do not you want freedom? The officer will show you freedom by word and also deed... Won't you sacrifice an old woman to the officer for a few hours? We sacrifice

*World Without Names*

our souls to protect you and your family, and to protect the homeland's border… How little you feel for your homeland!".

He then ordered the most difficult of all other torture methods I'd received.

"Tomorrow," he said, "you will bring the mother and the wife of this animal. Then, at ten at night, you'll gather for me all the single men and bring a liter of whisky. I want to be drunk with your wife and mother tomorrow, so, if you want, do not confess. Tomorrow, you'll bring me this animal without a face mask so he can see freedom with his own eyes. Do you want freedom or not??"

I shouted at them, "No! No! My mother's sick. I can confess everything you want, but do not hurt my mother".

My brother commented: "Definitely they do that. In the past they had done that and worse. Osman had heard some of what the other detainees discussed, and he could not bear this, and confessed to everything they wanted. Osman was not lucky. He was handed a difficult paper and told to confess to its content, and he signed".

I told my brother: "I do not understand."

My brother said: "It does not matter if you confess or not. The investigator has piles of papers printed with ready-made accusations. All he has to do is report daily to his leadership that he's captured people accused of such-and-such, and when the checkpoints bring detainees, he'll choose one group by chance, with whatever comes to his hand, giving a paper to the detainee who's been tortured with the Ghost in front of him for hours and saying: sign

*World Without Names*

this for your confession. Before signing, the detainee suffers in many sessions of torture such as I have told you about."

"So, they do not want names," I said.

"No. They want numbers. One time, imagine, they brought us a group of detainees wearing black t-shirts. When we asked what they were accused of, they said they did not know. We found out later that they were accused of wearing black t-shirts because there were orders to arrest a number of people who wore black. The reason was that people in one demonstration agreed to wear black, so they could know each other, and so the regime arrested everyone wearing black, even if they were only passing by in the street and had no connection to the demonstration. Wearing black was a reason to be arrested that day.

They want numbers, and, for every accusation, they want a number from the leadership. Osman was unlucky because he was accused of arming and killing members of the security apparatus, while on my paper, I was accused of demonstrating and sabotaging public property and insulting the president and raising the colonizers' flag.

Osman was miserable. He was tortured more than any of us. He was called by his name nearly every time the door clanked and people turned their faces to the walls. In the last period, they pushed him down stairs so that ligaments in his leg tore, and he could not get up any more, but they still insisted on calling his name. Another detainee had to sacrifice for him and receive his torture to allow him to rest. I sacrificed and was tortured for him several times. Every time, three torturers whipped me 300 times. These men have no idea what humanity means.

*World Without Names*

"Did the person who sacrificed for him ever confess instead of him as they tortured them for a confession?" I asked.

"No, no… They find a pleasure in torturing humans. They would come late at night to get twenty people to torture because the officer on duty would be drunk yet not sleepy, so he'd have fun with different types of torture even a demon could not devise."

My brother kept silent for a while, and then his forehead dropped into his palm, and he lifted his eyes a little.

"Imagine that once, one of the officers on duty had a nightmare, and he woke up frightened in his bed, calling out: 'Those dogs want to choke me. They want to choke me. Thirty of them sat on my chest and meant to choke me'. Then he shouted at the guards and torturers, ordering them around on that horrible night.

The door clanked, and everyone rushed and turned towards the walls as usual, and we heard his voice giggling.

He said: 'You're still sleeping, right? Too bad… We have a 5-star Meridien service here, right? Listen, you bastards, we've got new orders from the colonel. Tonight, thirty terrorists have to be executed. Later, thirty others among you who tried to harm the colonel in his nightmare will be wanted, so let them show themselves or we'll get them out. We know them one by one'.

Nobody moved. At that moment, we would've wished for the walls to break so that we could fly away. How we wished at that moment to die! A horrible silence hung over us for several seconds, and then a soft crying sounded, which spread to the others, before the guards' voice returned like an earthquake.

They said: 'Escape is not an option, got it? Okay then. Everyone who receives a blow to the head, leave immediately!'

Those were terrible moments. To wait, listening to the voice of the striker as he passed from one head to the next, was to be born again. But I was struck by that iron slap, and thus chosen amongst the thirty to be executed.

They took us out without giving us time to say goodbye or to leave a last will for our families, or to decide how to divide our possessions and clothes amongst those who were to live. We walked, tied together by a long chain that bound us all, to the courtyard full of masked faces.

"You thirty, get ready for an execution after a bit."

They put us on low chairs, but they did not tie up our hands. We stayed like statues next to each other in a row, and all of us were listening to the prayers of our neighboring inmates as their hearts beat rapidly in their chest. After a torturing handful of minutes, ropes dropped from above, and executioners started placing them around our necks. The main officer's voice shook the room:

"You're afraid, right? You still want to live even after you ravaged the country, and you also want to choke me, you bastards!"

He unleashed a flood of horrible curses we did not hear well, as we were making sure to say our last *shahadah*, "*There is no God but God and Muhammad is His Messenger*". One man from, I imagined, the bottom row, raised his voice and challenged the officer by reciting verses from the Qu'ran. The officer and his torturers went crazy, and he shouted:

"Are you calling on your Lord to save you? Let Him come and save you! Let me see Him! Let Him come! If He wanted you, He wouldn't have let you come here. The lord who can save you here is Mr. President, understand?'

We heard a strong punch, that sounded as if it took off a piece of his head.

"Who is your lord, you bastard?'

The man did not reply, but we heard the sounds of repeated punches accompanied by the question: 'Who is your lord, you bastard? Mr. President! The president!'

'I do not recognize your Lord!'

We heard the man's scream, and then he kept silent forever. I imagined the officer's voice saying, *'Let him die like a dog'*, then howled like a wolf, ordering: 'Carry out the executions!'.

The chairs were kicked out from under our feet from the start of the row. Yet the strange thing was that, with every kick to a chair, the man's screaming increased instead of being choked off. When the chair down my feet was kicked away, I found my hands, as a reaction, grabbing the rope above me so not let it snap my neck and leave my body float in mid-air.

It was a dirty game, as they'd left our hands free, hung between life and death. He whose hands untied the rope no doubt would choke, especially when the torturers struck him and shouted: 'Leave the rope, dogs, you definitely do not want to die! You want to live…'

The way that night ended was thousands of times worse than a real execution. They said that the officer wanted to have fun after his accursed nightmare, so he made up that game of death.

They did not want us to die at that moment because they did not want to lose the pleasure of torturing us."

My brother then turned to me. "Do you imagine a death harder than this psychological torture?

They dropped us and splashed us with hot water that burned our bare skin. Then they stroked our bodies with salt and said we could leave for the dorm and sleep in safety. Yet, how could someone whose wounds had been painted with salt taste the sweetness of sleep?

We went back, happy to be alive, as if we had been born again, but not all of us came back. Osman and I came back, but we lost some older people who could not manage seizing the rope. They must have choked. Our friends who were waiting their turn were postponed to the next day, and they lived a thousand deaths before their time of death finally arrived. They allowed us to sleep in their places, stretching out our whole bodies and taking their spots on the ground while they slept standing, awaiting their last moments to come.

* * *

"What happened to Osman?" I asked.

"They transferred him to Damascus before us. Yet we did not know that. He, like many others, went out and never came back. Some of those who left were transferred, and others died, while fewer were freed. What I want to say is that Osman went out and never came back, while I stayed. Then they transferred me, along with thirty others to the capital, as they transferred detainees in Idlib sixty days after their arrest.

They held us together like animals, with a long chain that bound our hands. They pushed us in, crammed masked faces in a closed car. We knew where they were driving us. But there was a surprise on the road: They gave everyone a whole loaf of bread, three pieces of falafel, and a tomato. Imagine that, for us, that was a five-star meal. It was very delicious!

"How was your food in the prison?" I asked.

My brother gave a bitter smile. "Food? We were around 300 and sometimes, after the clanking sound of the door that cut into our hearts, three packets of bread would be thrown to us, which meant less than forty loaves. Sometimes every detainee would have half a loaf".

"Only bread?"

"Sometimes they sent in potatoes, so that several people could share one piece.

If we were Ghosted in the courtyard, they would put us together on a skewer, just like the kind used to grill meat, and they would leave us for hours, maybe days, until our feet swelled up larger than our heads. The guard would pass and put some pieces of bread into the opened mouths. He gave us only small bites so that we wouldn't die of hunger. They wanted to torture us to the end. When they gave us some yogurt or rotten jam, we would find it a great act of grace.

In Damascus's Kafr Sosa, they moved us to Security Department 258. We were crammed in there, three stories underground. But there was less torture. From there, we would be moved to the courts, in accordance with the accusations against us. Some would be moved to the civil courts, which were the easiest courts, and others to field courts, where their sentences ranged from twenty years to life in prison. Some detainees were transferred to military courts, and those mostly wear red outfits allocated to those sentenced to death. From Kafr Sosa, detainees were transferred to the Palmyra prison or to Saydnaya. I went to Saydnaya, and I met Osman there again in the fourth dormitory. When I saw him for the first time, I ignored him, afraid that someone would notice us.

When we got a moment out of sight, we hugged each other. We hugged each other as though we were more than brothers. I discovered that he was being moved to a field court, since the accusations against him were arming and killing. He wept a lot that day and remembered his sick mother, who had been waiting months for her medicine.

In Saydnaya Prison, we experienced new forms of torture and pain, but the worst came from listening to the nighttime voices that penetrated ears and souls—screams of men pierced the night as they begged until death. One of the unforgettable voices was a woman's, as she screamed continuously until morning, repeating: 'I swear, Sir, I do not know anything about my husband. I swear I haven't seen him for a year.'

They insulted her with the sort of vile curses that any human with the minimum of emotion or kindness could never use. She kept silent sometimes, as though unconscious, and then we heard her asking for help among the drunken voices as though they were tearing apart her body.

## World Without Names

She screamed: 'I'm under your protection, shame on you, you cannot do this,' but there was the sound of giggling and reveling in their cups in that dark night. On other nights, we heard the voices of female guards, who were no different from their male colleagues, using the same cuss words their male counterparts did.

I can never forget the voices of the children. They brought children and tortured them in front of their mothers. They raped the mothers in front of their children or husbands or brothers or fathers."

It was then that I knew why Osman had confessed to what he did not do.

At a different time, my brother returned to the subject:

"When Osman knew I would be transferred from the field court to a civil one, as a result of presidential pardon, he begged me every day not to forget his mother, and to visit her. Reassure her. Many were in situations like Osman's, but we had no tools to keep the names and addresses of their families except in memory.

During the last period of my detention, they started to take better care of Osman than the others. They healed his wounds and the bruises on his face, as well as the deep injury in his cheek carved by the edge of the iron door he was slammed into. slam his head into iron door.

Osman was surprised by this sudden bout of care. Other detainees had a chance to see a doctor on Wednesday. They could not see his face, but he would sit at the iron window and call: Who is sick? They would raise their hands without turning their faces to the source of the voice. One treatment would be delivered to everyone, regardless of the problem or disease.

However, they started to treat Osman differently, and they would take him out for hours to heal his wounds. They also added some olives to his food rations, and sometimes an egg-sized yogurt. At this point, other detainees pulled away from him as they had their doubts, and they even feared him, thinking the prison authorities might have implanted him as a spy amongst them. But I knew Osman and his secret."

"What was the secret behind their care?" I asked. "And what was Osman's secret?"

"He told me that they were taking him out to train him for a TV show, to be broadcast widely, in which he would confess to crimes he'd committed. It would be evidence on how caring the government is for its people, and that criminals like Osman did not escape without punishment.

They forced him to memorize his lines word by word.

After four months in Saydanya, I left Osman. I tried to contact his mother, but my heart could not bear telling her the truth. I sent someone to tell her that Osman had disappeared in Damascus, and that he could not return home for fear of being arrested and recruited into military service. I also heard that one of the liars who was with us inside Saydnaya prison stole half a million Syrian pounds from Osman's family in exchange for a phone call."

"Would a call have been possible?" I asked.

"I do not think so," he said. "Your attempts might see the light of day if you have managed to secure an agreement with the prison's high officers, after paying them large amounts of money.

Careers are made from lies in exchange for millions of dollars. They would exploit people's willingness to sacrifice anything for their loved ones. I heard that Osman was sentenced to twenty years in prison. "

* * *

It was a strange coincidence that I learned details of Um Osman's story from my brother. Unfortunately, I could not fulfil my promise to his mother, despite acknowledging the pieces of information she wanted to know. This was for two reasons:

First, the TV show that had been in the work for months was broadcast and Um Osman immediately watched the episode. Second, after she saw the interview, Um Osman raced ahead of me to the other world.

Every day, the questions in my notebook grow:

What happened to Osman? Is he still alive in that hell?

Will he be transferred to another prison? Will he meet an old man who's been imprisoned for more than 40 years? Will he sit beside him and feel the old blood flowing in the old man's veins? Will he dare and hug a man he only met in the darkness of prisons?

*Will the prison walls, someday, confess all the secrets they have heard? As a believer, I deem that the oppressors will be judged eventually. Their very hands and legs will confess to the crimes they made before they are even sent to prison.*

*Why do generations in my country only meet in the narrow prison caves?*

*Was my homeland too unendurable to cradle them in its vastness?*

*What happened to those thousands of people filling the world to its brim? Weren't our youths supposed to build a new homeland? Who would reconstruct our country in their absence? The rulers and oppressors? Are these even worthy of this piece of heaven on Earth?*

*What would the fate of the millions of children be, those angels born waiting for their names to come from fathers forcibly disappeared and turned into mere numbers? Day after day, questions piled up in my notebook. But what of answers? Where must I search for the words to silence my buzzing brain?*

# From the Days of Siege

## Passing Through Death

The period that started in October of 2016 was known as the Second Siege of Aleppo. These unforgettable days will remain deeply engraved in my memory, as will the pain I suffered in those difficult days.

We arrived in besieged Aleppo with the aid vehicles, entering through Kafr Hamra, the only way to cross into the entire city, whether besieged or liberated. There were huge crowds of cars waiting to cross safely. I realized that only 900 meters remained between us and the city where thousands of hungry people dreamt of tasting a loaf of bread, even if it were mere arid crisps.

We stopped our cars by the side of the street and got out to see what was going on. I understood from conversations here and there that the way ahead of us was named Castillo Road. This road was marked by snipers and rocket launchers coming from the area of New Aleppo, as well as other areas. No one could pass without being caught by the snipers.

The smell of death poured off the road as it stretched out like a terrifying snake, in adjacency to a dirt barrier that ran in parallel with a two-meter-high wall, such that small cars could sometimes hide and sometimes move, quick as an arrow, entering or exiting the city according to orders that came from the checkpoints at both ends. Big vehicles like the aid trucks had to wait for the snipers to sleep in order to avoid their watchful eyes.

*From the Days of Siege*

I felt outraged as I contemplated the cars' load. We weren't carrying bombs, bullets, or explosive materials to kill people. We only carried food for the hungry people hiding inside away from bullets, bombs, and rockets. Perhaps they did not belong to any of the warring parties fighting to control their city of birth and the streets in which they grew up as children. People struggled to seek out their living and secure their children's future. I imagine them now, in the deep shelters, hugging their scared children quivering from the sounds of bombs and screaming with hungry fear. Yes, they cried out from hunger, and they might die while the aid vehicles filled with food helplessly stood only 900 meters away.

*What a jungle the world is! The crimes of the sniper who watches the road do not only amount to shooting passersby. They are responsible for mercilessly killing thousands of children, without shooting one bullet, by preventing milk from reaching their gaping mouths. Oh God, what has war made of these creatures called human beings?*

The spirit of adventure possessed me, urging me to enter, to reach those besieged people, to relieve their pain. One of the missions I had was to assess the people's needs inside Aleppo, and later convey them to the parties intending to help them. I had no time to lose. I had to find a way to enter.

I knew that cars carrying fuel, like gasoline and diesel, were the most adventurous in crossing the road that was watched by death at every inch. Fuel vehicles had to supply bakeries, as without them they would stop working. Hospitals also depended on diesel instead of electricity, which had become an edifice of the past.

*From the Days of Siege*

I had to find the driver of a fuel tanker to help me enter. It was not difficult to find one, as dozens of cars were at the side of the road, waiting for a chance to enter. But the hard thing was convincing the driver.

I chose a man in his sixties, sitting alone beside a large tanker. His eyes were fixed on his wireless radio, which buzzed from time to time, announcing the launch of a helicopter, or the start of a rocket launcher or machine gunner. It was dark. He was greedily inhaling at his cigarette as I approached. He was immersed in his wireless, trying to comprehend the intermittent words. When I addressed him with my request, he did not answer right away, rather ruminating upon my words for a while before asking me to sit down. He then began explaining to me the seriousness of the adventure awaiting me.

"Do you know what it means to enter in a fuel tanker?" the driver said.

"It means it's a big car and the dirt barrier won't hide it from the sniper's gaze," I said.

"Also, do you know the danger of what I'm carrying?" he asked.

"What do you mean?"

"We carry flammable materials, meaning that any bullet that to hit us will ignite the car and we'll be burned within minutes, before anyone comes to help."

Even though I was afraid, my desire to reach the people was bigger than my fear.

"Lives are in the hand of God, uncle," I said. "Nothing will happen to us but what God has written."

He looked at me, admiring what I said. "God's word is the truth".

"Is your entry urgent?" he asked.

Without hesitation, I said: "Yes, there's someone waiting for me."

"Your family?"

I did not know what to tell him. Those people were my family, but not the family that had given birth to me. Every frightened woman inside was my mother. Every child that needed me was my brother. I wanted to explain their needs to those who could fulfil them. Those people were my family. They were from me, and I was from them. So I said without giving it another thought:

"Yes!"

Then, to further convince him to take me with him, I told him: "I work with a humanitarian organization, and I'm required to enter to see what people need there".

He looked at me again for a long time, as though checking me from head to toe, as if the word "organization" had worked against me, as though he would give me an answer way beyond my expectations.

"My son, our way is dangerous and it's a heavy responsibility. I do not mind picking you up, but it's your responsibility, not mine." He stressed the words *your responsibility.*

I said without hesitation: "It's my responsibility, you got it".

*From the Days of Siege*

He agreed and asked me to wait until they allowed us to enter. "I think we won't be late—the diesel I carry is for a field hospital, and they insist on letting me enter as soon as possible, as the engines that run the hospital's machine might stop if the fuel runs out".

I told my colleagues that I will go ahead with the fuel tanker and wait for them inside. Even though they condemned my quick decision, I was stubborn headed, and I went back to wait with the driver. It was almost midnight.

He asked me not to walk far away. They might open the road at any moment.

"How long will it take to pass?"

Without giving it much thought, he said "Minutes and not more, if God makes it easy."

We waited hours, or maybe days, to pass a distance that should've taken no more than three minutes. I returned to my reflections, contemplating the darkened fuel tank.

"You're working with a humanitarian organization, right?" the driver asked.

"Yes."

He sighed.

*"Is there any humanity left, my son? It died. Humanity should be put in museums."* He then pointed to the fuel tank. "Do you see this tank? Every drop inside is connected with the soul of a human being who might die if it does not reach its destination. We're forced to wait here until the sniper goes away

*From the Days of Siege*

to put on the teapot or to pee, and then we will be able to reach the people whose lives depend on us.

*"Snipers can kill a lot of people unknowingly. Killing is not confined to penetrating the body with bullets. It's enough for the sniper not to allow this tank of fuel that's needed by a hospital waiting for us minutes away. Do you know how many people during these minutes will die, not to forget those killed by the warring parties? If the fuel in the engine runs out, how many children will die in their incubators? How many patients will die in operating rooms? How many people depending on oxygen will suffocate?"*

He sighed from the deepest chambers of his chest. I felt the warmth of his sigh getting torn by the sounds of bombing. From time to time, tracer bullets penetrated the darkness. He said as though talking to himself, "The world abandoned its humanity long ago. Beasts do not do what humans do nowadays. I swear they do not".

At 3: 00 in the morning., the crossing point opened, and the first car was allowed to pass. I do not know where the sniper had gone. I did not think about him at that moment; I was shaking uncontrollably for those first few minutes. After a while, the sniper began occupying my thoughts. Was it a change in the killing shifts? Or had he just gone to pee and, during that time, thousands of those awaiting fuel tankers and aid would be allowed to live again? Or maybe it was a phone call received from the woman he loves, and they were flirting in the stunning April atmosphere. He might tell her how proud he was to kill the very many he shot that day. I even imagined them arguing about the names of the children they'd have in the future, or how many of them there would be. And the longer the disagreement continued, the more lives would be allowed to continue through the crossing.

170

*From the Days of Siege*

The first car that passed was a Suzuki that could hide itself behind the tad-higher dirt barrier. One man occupied the front seat whereas the backseats sat a woman and a child. The car zapped like an arrow through the darkness, with no regard for the holes in the road that caused the car to bounce. Behind it, the second car set off with a number more passengers.

Uncle Abu Abdo was ready behind the engine. We were fifth in line. Three cars had already passed safely. He spoke reassuringly, as though he'd he has noticed my pallid confusion:

"Do not be afraid. You're on the barrier side. If anything happens, open the door and shelter yourself by the barrier. If you hear the sound of a bullet, jump out right away." He went on. "If you hear the bullet, it won't kill you. *The bullet that kills you is the one you do not hear.*" He laughed, despite the difficult moment.

As the three cars set off in front of us, I calmed down a little. For the first time, I was aware that I was on the right side of the car and the driver was on the left, and that, less than half a meter away, stood the most dangerous place near the embankment.

*In war, the measure of time and space becomes very precise—from one second to another, between one meter and the other, there could be the distance separating life and death.*

Before our car could start its journey, something we all feared happened.

Heavy gunfire broke the silence, and I heard bullets whizzing above our heads. It was a matter of seconds before we were down on the ground, and

*From the Days of Siege*

the night's clouds receded, allowing us to distinguish the people around us filling the air with their screams.

Oh God, be with us, Oh Lord! I saw the fourth car catch fire, as though it had been hit by incendiary materials. I did not notice what it was carrying when it passed by us. But, by the light of the fire, I could see firefighters sneaking in alongside the barrier and moving the people screaming from inside the burnt car. And the fifth car was ours…

We did not receive the order to move right away, but it was not late before the road was declared safe again. Maybe the sniper went back to his call, and he could send a snapshot of himself after shooting the ashen car. Maybe it was enough for him to show his super heroism and his skill-full hunting of the charred bodies.

Minutes and not more passed before Abu Abdo started our journey and headed toward the ticking clock. He was a hero indeed, "Oh God, we rely on you!"

He stepped on the pedal, causing the tank to emit the roar of a terrifying monster. He went and challenged Death. And it was as he said. Three minutes.

Three minutes! Each minute consisted of 60 seconds. And between each pair of seconds, there was a vast world, with space for the orbit of fantasies and dreams that stumbled with the terrified heartbeats accelerating with every meter travelled. I cannot describe him except as a hero. Tons of air were imprisoned in my chest, refusing to get out. We passed near the burnt car, and then we were in the darkness of the last third of the road. Any crackling beside the tank would lead to an explosion. Any movement would shake the earth out of its orbit. It is I who was shaking badly. I never felt as cold. My eyes stared at Abu Abdo's clenched lips, which resembled his fisted hands gripping the steering wheel. He looked at me through the tail of his eye as he slowed down. It was a long time between the moment he opened his lips and when he said, "Thank God for our safety, my son."

Despite the total darkness, I felt the sun filling the whole universe with its filtering rays, seeping into my freezing entrails. I finally relaxed and released the clouds of imprisoned air.

"We made it?"

I whispered, as though I were pronouncing the first words in my life. I was inside Aleppo, but the aid cars had stayed, still waiting for their chance outside.

I heard Uncle Abu Abdo saying, "We're safe now."

## Where is My City?

So said Abu Abdo. I remembered this sentence, which was at that moment the gospel of my birth. The genesis of my being. How painful these words were to remember while I was wandering in the streets of Aleppo.

I have known those streets since childhood, and I had not been gone for long. I had left just a few months before, not more, but everything had changed. This was not the Aleppo I knew.

The streets I knew were those full of life in motion. You could not find room to walk between the noisy cars. The voices of shopkeepers and street vendors would be buzzing in the air around you. But now they were almost

*From the Days of Siege*

as empty as a ghost town. Even the faces I saw were strange and grim, as though they have come from some other unknown world.

The day after we entered, the crossing point we passed through was blocked, after the aid vehicles had entered.

During the twenty days I spent under siege, I learned things I would not have gained in a lifetime. I intentionally visited the neighborhoods I lived in before. With every visit, whatever life in my heart twinkled away. Not only the faces have left, but also the entire soul of Aleppo.

Here was Uncle Abu Ali's shop. There, he'd been sitting on his wooden chair every morning. But now, there is neither the shop nor the chair nor Abu Ali.

In the place of that huge hill of rubble from destroyed houses, there had been a huge square where we often played football. Now, it was a mountain of rock debris, trash, and iron wires.

There was a building where an acquaintance of mine had lived. We'd call him from the street, and he would appear on the third-floor balcony before coming down. Yes, it had been a three-story building, but now I saw nothing in front of me but roofs on broken pillars that touched the ground on one side, while the other side hung by its iron wires.

But strangest of all was that the first few inhabitants I bumped into did not know fear. They were walking quickly in the street, indifferent to the warplanes roaring as they flew above them, or the deafening sounds of bombing. They lived their daily lives as though they were in a different

*From the Days of Siege*

world—different from the one they walked in—seemingly indifferent to everything going on around them.

Perhaps they had nothing to be afraid of. They went on with their lives as though they were watching a horror film, and everything happening around them was only acting. The projected state of cynicism was confirmed by a group of people I saw, playing in a square beside a pile of trash. The game was called *al-hah*: every child grabbed a stick. A smaller stick was placed in a hole. The player would hit the small stick using his   own, trying to get it to move as far as possible. The player was allowed to hit the stick three times. He would hit the small stick with the side of his own stick, and when the small stick flew in the air he would hit it again, following it like an arrow.

The player would then run after the stick, indifferent to a helicopter's roar as it dropped a barrel bomb, or a Sukhoi jet emptying its rockets. The game's joy was greater than all other sounds, especially when a boy hit the small stick successfully, and drove it far away. He would stand, stretching up to his full, little height, proud of his triumph. He would show off his soft muscles and stare at the jets, shouting as he flexed his fists: *We are the heroes. We are the heroes!* The other children would repeat after him: *We are the heroes. We are the heroes!*

## I wrote in my notebook:

Everything I saw during the siege days in Aleppo was painful. But what hurt me more were people's requests. I was supposed to get to know their needs, to report them to the charities, so they could help them.

In the past, Aleppo has been a dominant force in trade and industry, its name shining in international markets. So what did the Aleppans ask for today?

Aleppo, that dreamy city that used to race to wake up in the morning, had now fallen into a deep slumber. When I met people and asked them about their needs, bread and water were their dreams.

Some said: We do not want anything. All we want is for the warplanes and bombs to leave, and for the war to stop, and then we can manage our lives.

They were drying out bread in fear of the days to come, and they removed the water tanks from their roofs after becoming full of shrapnel, and put them in what was left of their homes.

## In a field hospital

With great difficulty, I managed to reach the field hospital. At the time, it was still working. Most other hospital services were rendered out of service after being shelled. Even though I had a friend to guide me—a young person who helped people for the sake of God without awaiting gratitude—it was not easy for me to find the hospital. Without the fast cars and their horns heading to the hospital, I would not have been able to reach it, for many reasons: the streets have changed, many buildings have been lost, and the place where they chose to relocate the hospital could not have been predicted.

It had been built in a neighborhood where most of the adjacent buildings had been destroyed. The building where the hospital was housed was not

*From the Days of Siege*

meant to be a hospital—it was barely larger than a residence. It was two stories tall. One of them was used as a storm room. I knew they had been forced to choose such a place because it did not attract attention, and thus less likely to find itself under the aerial bombardments that targeted medical centers and field hospitals.

Unluckily, I entered the hospital at the same time that the ambulances arrived, carrying injured people pulled from under the rubble.

The hospital was dynamic, a busy buzzing beehive, a public market. The suffering voices of the newly injured overlapped with the moans of their families, especially the mothers. Their cries were heartbreaking.

From the first step one would take into its foyer up until its last room, no empty space would be left. Even in corridors, you would find injured people laying amid pools of their own blood, while a nurse or a volunteer would be helping them, trying to stop the bleeding until a doctor—who would be busy with another one of the injured—could come and check on them. How many fathers and mothers carried their injured children and ran here and there searching for help!

What caught my attention was the serenity of the staff, and the slowness of their movements compared with the agitation of the people, and the cries of distress of the injured people's companions. I knew they were used to dealing with such cases, as they lived amidst it every day. Bombs and jets hit the area continuously, and injured people arrived unceasingly because most of the other field hospitals had been hit and could no longer serve the injured.

After more than two hours, I managed to meet with the doctor in charge. Despite his wide welcoming smile, he was exhausted and sweating. He apologized to me after I introduced myself and reminded him of the doctors who referred him to me.

Exhausted, he sat in a chair and wiped at the sweat on his bald head with a canvas handkerchief. His baldness spread from the middle of his head snow white beard. Yet he seemed to be hardly older than thirty.

"Sorry I was late. We had urgent operations that could not be postponed."

"Were the results good, God willing?"

"We do the best we can, under the present circumstances. As you see, my friend, we do our duty and the rest is in God's hands."

"Sure. May God give you strength. No doubt that God will reward you."

"We do not ask for rewards from anyone but God. Do you know that most of our staff members are volunteers?"

"No doubt they have previous medical experience."

"Some of them, yes. Others, we trained them. We sometimes need double the number of the staff on hand." He smiled and continued. "Do you know that some of the staff members have only a degree in nursing, but today their experience is equal to that of specialized doctors?"

"Because of the large number of cases they see."

"Because we're forced to deal with a lot of cases. Sometimes a staff member might be forced to perform a surgical procedure on someone who needs urgent help and is about to die. Mostly they're successful. Most things learned in medical school cannot be applied here. Or, if they can, many of the injured would die in your hands."

*From the Days of Siege*

I remember an interesting story from the beginning of the revolution: There was a knock at my door after midnight, so I told myself 'God save me, no doubt it is the intelligence forces'. I was surprised when two masked men pushed themselves inside before I'd invited them in. One of them said, 'Doctor, we ask help from you and from God'. Then they removed their masks, and I recognized one of the men, as he was my patient from a nearby village. After they stammered a while, I came to understand that a brother of one of them had been injured in a demonstration, receiving more than one bullet in his side. They did not dare take him to a hospital, so they wanted me to help him at home. I carried my bag and rode on a motorbike to reach their house."

A smile lingered for quite a while on the doctor's face.

"Imagine that they hid him in a stable, in fear of the security force raids. They wanted me to perform an operation there. I performed neither diagnosis nor sterilization. But the operation was successful. The patient is still alive. God is the healer."

I understood that, in this hospital, they worked in conditions similar to those in his story. When I asked him to write down what they needed, he wrote a lot of things—enough to establish a whole hospital, ranging from machines for radiology to echocardiography, to alcohol and cotton. When I went out, I looked one last time at the building, and I thought about writing in my notebook that *the hospital needed another real hospital, starting from the building, to equipment, and ending with the staff.*

## With the rescue team

In times of war, you would deem any place you go to as *the* best portrayal of the Syrian tragedy. This is what I thought when I walked in destroyed and abandoned streets. Here, you can see the war and all its remaining scars with your naked eyes. When I visited field hospitals, I thought they contained all the tragedies of the war, but then I changed my mind and realized that working with rescue teams was in fact the epitome of misery. There, you come in contact with injuries and tragedies directly, in the first moments they occur. You hear the first screams and see the first shock. I still cannot forget the man who stood desperate as we lifted his whole family from under rubble. It was an unforgettable day.

It was a day from the siege of Aleppo, when I was forced to stay in the city, as all crossing points that connected it with the outer world were closed.

I remembered my friend Ahmad, my fellow student at school who came from my same neighborhood. After we lost contact for more than two years, he told me that he had recently joined the Syria Civil Defense forces to rescue civilians in Aleppo. Ahmad was a rebellious boy. He always was a high-spirited handsome young man, a buzzing bee in my class. The teacher would often give him dozens of notices for his chitter-chats that always got him in trouble. But people liked him. And he was nothing of a lazy student. However, from the very first demonstrations, he stopped going to school, was keen to attend every protest, chanting in the first row and hoisted on people's shoulders.

Pictures of him were circulated, and these reached the regime. His family knew he would be arrested, so they tried to hide him. After two years, I got a phone call from him at the Syrian-Turkish border. This was the first time I talked to him after his long absence. It was also the last. I learned from him that he was working in Aleppo with the Syria Civil Defense teams. As usual, he talked like a storm. I understood that he adored his work and considered it a holy act. More than once, he recited me a verse from the Quran.

*"And that if a person saves a man from death, it will be as if he had saved the whole of mankind."*

He asked me to visit him in Aleppo, and I promised that I would search for him the moment I would arrive to Aleppo. When I asked him about his address, he laughed in a manner I will never forget.

"You won't have to search long to find the Civil Defense teams, as we're the first people to reach the places hit during bombardments. Some even say that we know about the strikes before they happen, as if we're making them up. This is what many news reports claim."

He added: "Look at the places hit by jets, and you'll know from the dirt clouds that form where to head, and you'll find our teams are already there. *The dirt cloud is the address of the Civil Defense."* Ahmad was right, but I was too late. I did not find him. I was late by only a few days, not more.

Reaching their address was not difficult, as they were in every location. Very soon after a jet hit an area, you would hear sirens of their vehicles whistling like wind as they headed toward the targeted area before the cloud of dirt drifted away.

I reached their center before evening. It was located next to a school that had been previously hit. Education ceased to be when students' blood got mixed with the ink from their papers. When their notebooks became dyed with crimson red.

*From the Days of Siege*

They were housed in the semi-dark basement. Sunlight snuck in through rectangular windows along the ceiling. The acidic smell of moisture, socks, and the remains of food permeated the space. Dozens of iron beds were scattered along. On the walls of the basement that resembled those of a prison, some memories were scribbled in unclear letters. Old clothes and white helmets were hung. It was from this humid grave that they set off like the wind to offer life to other people.

I asked the head of the team, Abu Zaid, about my friend Ahmad. By chance, he was the first one I met, and Ahmad had been close to him. He did not reply directly, but I saw the answer in a tear lingering inside his eyes. I discovered that Ahmad had been martyred just a few days before, while trying to rescue a victim.

I decided quickly, as usual, to work with the team in Ahmad's place, as long as I was trapped in Aleppo. When I spoke to Abu Zaid about my decision, he was more than welcoming.

Yet, what happened after the rest of the team got back from their mission and met me was something else. Abu Zaid introduced me to the team and said I would be working with them. Their opinions on this varied. Some welcomed me, some kept silent with neutral smiles, but there was a small guy called Jako who really annoyed me. Hostility showed in his first look, and he denied my existence. He asked me, doubtingly, as though underestimating my abilities: "Do you know how dangerous it is to do the work **we** do?"

"I can learn from you," I said, smiling.

"We took classes to be able to do this work."

"I'll do what you ask of me."

"You'll cause trouble for us, and we do not know you. Maybe you work for…" Then he winked and laughed in a silly way. For a long time, he tried to make the others laugh, too.

I felt rage against that boy circulating through my veins. He was young—not more than 17—and although his features seemed childish, deep inside his eyes I saw a malice that belied his gentle features. I wished I could grab his from his clothes and shout:

"Why do you want to stop me from helping people? You're no better than me. I have been a part of many humanitarian projects, and I serve people just like you do," but Abu Zaid's angry voice brought the situation to a closure when he blurted out a warning.

"Jako!"

This mere word was enough to cut off Jako's hysterical laughter, as though he'd been slapped across the face. Abu Zaid continued:

"This is a friend of the martyr Ahmad, and you know Ahmad, so why do you doubt him? May God's mercy find Ahmad, who was the best and most courageous among us."

The team members whispered, asking God to bestow His mercy upon Ahmad's soul.

"And remember," Abu Zeid said. "It's not your job to accept or refuse people, Jako. That's my job."

*From the Days of Siege*

Jako withdrew to his bed in a faraway corner, and there he got out his mobile and started playing with it without uttering a single word. Abu Zaid took my hand, asking me to disregard and forgive Jako's doubts, as sometimes regime collaborators did try to join them.

I told him that I knew about such cases.

He guided me to an empty bed that would be mine for the duration of my stay. I did not ask to whom it already belonged. However, I felt that the dark-colored sponge mattress and the white helmet hanging on the wall had belonged to Ahmad.

When Abu Zaid sat beside me, I asked how Ahmad was martyred.

He gave a long sigh that ended in a moan.

"He was, may God have mercy on him, very impulsive and hot-blooded. He was always out front, ahead of others.

He told me about this a lot, but I heard only a little. I remembered Ahmad's features and his devious jokes and quarrels. I remembered seeing him hoisted on people's shoulders in the demonstrations as he chanted enthusiastically." Abu Zaid spoke sadly about the same things I remembered in Ahmad. He later tried teaching me some of the principles of rescue work.

"I was always telling him: 'Ahmad! The safety of the team is the most important thing in rescue work because if the team is bombed, it means death of everyone.' But he did not listen. Often, the jet would return to bomb the same place it had targeted before, hitting the rescuing teams and the gathering that was caused by the first bombardment.

*From the Days of Siege*

This was what happened to us as we were rescuing a family, and Ahmad was trying to remove a child from beneath the rubble. The child was calling out, his hands reaching out to Ahmad's when the jet came back. At that time, we had to leave and hide in the nearest shelter, but Ahmad did not leave. He kept holding the child's hand amidst the rubble. When we came back, we found him hugging the child, who was alive, but Ahmad was martyred."

Abu Zaid has just finished this story when the wireless walkie-talkies in everyone's hands began to cry out:

"Helicopter with barrel bombs was on the way to a target. Helicopter….barrel bombs." This sentence was repeated a lot. But the team members acted as though they did not hear a thing. Maybe they'd grown used to hearing such warning. However, all stood up upon hearing the word: "Aleppo! Aleppo! Helicopters inbound".

When they heard the word "inbound," the white helmets were on their heads and Abu Zaid was the first among them. I voiced out my desire to accompany them.

"You can relax today," Abu Zaid said. "Things are always like this. We always have work. You'll get your turn tomorrow." Abu Zaid laughed. "Do not worry, we have plenty of work. Unfortunately…."

I slept that night in the martyr's bed. In the darkness of the basement, his face circled around me, snatching sleep from my eyelids. I imagined the smile that never left his face dyed with the crimson red that covered his body getting lifted from under the rubble. I fell asleep at some point, as I was remembering his last words to me: "*And that if a person saves a man from death, it will be as if he had saved the whole of mankind.*" When I fell asleep, I

*From the Days of Siege*

saw him flying in green forests over palaces of marble, beneath which rivers flowed.

\* \* \*

There really was a lot of work. The jets did not stop their roaring, and the walkie-talkies did not keep silent. Death inhabited every corner of that besieged city.

I was still sleep-deprived from the previous night, and the next day was full of tragedies. It was Friday. I woke up to the team members' hassle while putting on their clothes. Most of them slept fully clothed. They shouted alerts at each other. Even though I did not hear the sound of the walkie-talkies, I understood they were heading to a place that had been targeted. The sun was barely peaking from its darkness, and the morning still stung sleepy faces with its cold April breeze. I put on the helmet that was hanging above my bed, and I followed Abu Zaid, who told me to go with him.

His eyes scanned the sky. Smoke was blowing over three places not far from us. We set out in more than one car, heading to the three check-points monitored by Abu Zaid and other observers. I was in Abu Zaid's car and the so-called Jako was with us. We arrived at an old neighborhood, one of those that had been haphazardly built and destroyed. It was an unorganized area in al-Shaar neighborhood, in the Tariq al-Bab district, as I expected. We passed through a street in which all of the buildings sitting on one side were in shambles. The hit target was an old three-storey building. A single family lived in the house. A man, his wife and five children, as well as the man's elderly parents. This was what we understood from the man who was screaming at the top of his lungs: "Oh God, oh God! God is the greatest!

*From the Days of Siege*

They're all gone, they're all gone!". I learned from the neighbors who gathered nearby that he was the owner of the home.

It was not only children screaming, but everyone else joined in the panic frenzy. You could barely understand a word being said. If you were to look at the bombed building, you would not know where to find the entrance. Everything laid under three piled ceilings. The top ceiling's front side had slid to the bottom of the second floor, while its back side was collapsed on the first floor. Pillars stretched up into the sky. The stairs that had bound them was suspended in the air. My colleagues climbed through the rubble that poured out in the streets, directly toward the second floor. I followed them. The overlapping walls and blocked corridors ended up pushing us back into the street. When we asked for directions, people withdrew in fear, except for a 40-year old man who was hitting his head with both fists and shouting from the depths of his aching heart: "Oh God! Oh God! All of them are gone!"

He was running towards the pile of rubble, trying to move aside pieces of ashen cement. Hopelessness would assail him, and he would strike his head again and scream, begging: "God! God!". I knew that this man was the owner of the house, and that it was his elderly parents, wife, and five children who were suffocating beneath its rubble. It was his fate to have gone outside not more than a half an hour before the bombardment, perhaps to bring them breakfast.

He was screaming: "I wish I were with you! I wish I had not gone out and I'd died with you instead! Oh God, who is there with me now?"

*From the Days of Siege*

The team was working with unparalleled effort, regardless of the simple tools they used. I was working with them when someone noticed my confusion. "Do like me," he said.

Despite their persistence, they were working with great care, fearing that the cement mass might collapse on those who might still be alive under the rubble.

To my awe, Jako was also removing pieces of rubble and continuously searching here and there for a remaining sign of life. In that moment, I felt how much I wronged Jako. He was pouring all his heart into the rescue work, as if the people under the rubble were his own family. He would not stop encouraging his fellow co-workers: "Come on, guys! Come here! You go there! Quickly, my brothers! Quickly!"

And then he shouted at the man who was pulling his beard and striking his head: "Uncle! Let God deal with it! God willing, we will get them out alive! Ask God and pray for us! We will get them out, we will!". But more than an hour had passed, and we had not found anyone.

Then, when we lifted the remains of a wall from the street, a crawlspace opened before us. It led us to find the bodies of the grandfather and grandmother. Meanwhile, one of us saw the first girl, who'd been thrown to the neighboring roof, and was dead. Then, the walkie-talkies alerted us to flee from the place, as the jets were coming back to bombard the region again.

After hours of work, and running back and forth between the consecutive air raids, a staff member shouted for help from a corner that seemed, from his choked voice, located far away. We understood that they had found the other children, all three of whom had been sleeping next to each other, as

*From the Days of Siege*

though they had not yet woken up that morning. They died, suffocated under the crushed ceiling, before they even woke up from their dreams.

The image of that father will be carved into my conscience for the rest of my life. He was standing beside the pile of rubble that had been, only a short time before, his cozy sweet home. He followed us with his unmoving gaze as the bulldozer shaved away the debris, searching for any protruding limb that might appear with every shave. From time to time, he would come to count the dead bodies on his fingers as though he'd lost his mind while gesturing to the bags: "These are five, my mom, dad, Raghad, Abdo, Fatima, and Sahar, but where is Munir? Where…? These are five so there are still two left, in addition to my wife". He would go back to counting again, forgetting that the first girl we found on the neighboring roof had been moved to a hospital.

In the depth of the rubble, near the remains of a circular staircase that I thought led to the first floor, I heard something similar to a moan. I tried concentrating on what I was hearing. It was a choked, intermittent moaning coming from below. We gathered to search for a way to reach the source of that voice.

After several minutes of digging, a hole appeared through the iron wires and masses of cement. The hole led to what looked like a kitchen. A woman was trapped inside. A gas smell began filling the place.

Abu Zaid replied to the woman's moans: "Mother, do not be afraid, do not! We've reached you! We've reached you!"

But there was still a far distance to reach the woman, and the smell of gas was overwhelming us. Suddenly, the walkie-talkies began screeching:

"Russian warplanes have entered the area and are headed to their target... clear the area. More than one Russian warplane has entered the target area."

I did not understand much of the message, but it seemed the area we were working in was a target. Like threads of lightning, we began evacuating the building from all sides. The warplane's roar raging through the sky almost ruptured my eardrums. I saw the rest of the team opening a shop— they dragged its huge door up and, in seconds, we were inside and the door was closed. I was about to say that we had left the woman alive and she almost certainly would be suffocated by the gas smell, but I remembered Abu Zaid's words from the day before:

"The safety of the team is the most important thing. If the team is injured, then everyone will die."

We were inside the dark shop. It was not really a shop, but rather an empty warehouse. A three-wheeled vehicle and an old box were standing in the corner.

It had caught my eye, as we ran toward the shop to take shelter, that several people had been moving around the building. I said to the person beside me, "If those people helped us, we would have finished the work quickly. But they were just watching".

He told me that, if I were to ask for help, they would definitely answer: "This is not our work, it's the Civil Defense business."

"But they can help, and God's hand is with us."

*From the Days of Siege*

"No, my brother. They might help in the last moments to hold a woman or a girl, or maybe they'll start helping after we finish our work to dig for what can be stolen."

"I do not understand."

"They're thieves, thieves. They have no ethics, no humanity. They wait for a dead woman to be lifted from under the rubble, then they rush to her, pretending to help so that they can rob her of a bracelet or ring. They rescue gold, not souls. They are thieves, do you understand?"

Oh God, how great is the scale of human contradictions! While a team is risking the lives of its members to save a life, there are others waiting on a corpse to rob its gold. While the door was crackling under the bombing pressure, potentially falling into its wrecked destiny above our own heads, one of the team members got up in the vehicle and held his mobile screen as far as his stretched arms and laughed, saying, "We'll take a goodbye selfie".

*I was not surprised by how they all laughed, as the horrors of death had no impact on them. Death had lost its force as they grew accustomed to its presence amongst them. They really were heroes. How I wished to stay with them!*

The second bombing noise was travelling across the street, close to the door. A split second before silence reigned, a team member tried dragging the door up, but the moment he heard fragments colliding on the street, he rushed to close it again.

The warplanes announced the end of their mission and headed back to base. Immediately, we were all jumping with joy and climbing the piles of the

*From the Days of Siege*

destroyed building as though nothing had happened. Abu Zaid was communicating with the second sub-team on the walkie-talkie, asking them to head towards our location immediately.

I thought he wanted them to come and help, but later I understood that three other houses on the same side of this street were just hit. The street outside was empty, except for the dirt that blocked our vision. What amazed me was the man we left in the destroyed home. Despite the rockets that dropped around him, he did not move from his place, and yet his fate was not to be injured. He was trying to reach the window to get to his suffocating wife.

We helped him stand afar so we could finish our job. He went back to the bags of corpses to count them again: "Sahar...my mom, dad......"

The first thing the team did was to drop an oxygen container so the woman would not asphyxiate.

It was difficult to reach her, especially that the use of an electric device to cut through the iron was not possible at the moment because any spark would ignite the leaked gas. Regardless, the team managed to cut the wires with regular saws with nothing but their rigid persistence and strong insistence. They cooperated—every one taking a turn without stopping for a second---to move the iron away and managed to eventually reach the woman.

She was still alive, but her pelvic bones and legs were broken. They held her in a specific way and participated in carrying her through the crawlspace. I heard her husband following her, saying in a soft voice: "Cover her up, my sons. Cover her up."

*From the Days of Siege*

At that moment, the men who were hovering around us came to help us carry the woman and the corpses to the car. I heard my friend Abu Zaid, who has just spoken to me about thieves, roaring at them:

"Thank you for your help, but kindly stay away for your safety's sake! May God reward you for your goodness." One man approached the team as if he had not heard my friend, so Abu Zaid reiterated, this time with a hint of acerbic irony: "I told you to go away. We do not want your help."

"Let me help you!"

"Go away, or I'll behead you with this saw and put you in a bag and carry you with them… Do you understand?"

Then, I saw the man retreat, frightened,: "We only wanted to do a good deed."

My friend turned to me and saw me listening to their discussion. "I see this man everywhere I go to rescue people. I know him well. Very well. He would even steal kohl from a person's eyes."

I heard the injured woman whisper in a scarcely audible voice: "My children, my children! Where are my children?"

"They're okay, auntie!" a voice said. "They're waiting for you!"

I asked myself where the children were in fact waiting. No doubt, they were waiting for her in heaven, and she might follow them soon.

While we were passing debris in the corner of a room, I saw what looked like a boy's foot buried under the shards, except for its naked toes. I began

*From the Days of Siege*

digging around the foot until the soft cold body appeared. Half of the back head was smashed. My friend lifted the little body, and I stood behind him.

For the first time, I was *face to face* with the Death that I feared. I saw it embodied in a girl whose head was smashed, her bones broken. I was the nearest one, so he handed the body to me to continue his way amidst the rubble. He called out: "We got the girl. Anyone else here?"

"Take her outside."

I turned away and stumbled on the piles of stone. My legs slipped right and left, but they kept moving, while my heart beat intensely up to an extent I thought it would wither in my chest. I avoided looking at the girl's face. I did not know if it was her body pulsating or my hands carrying her.

One colleague saw me confused, hardly seeing my way forward, so he swooped in like a falcon and got the girl from me.

"Give her to me, give her to me."

I not only felt that her weight moved off my forearms, but I also felt a mass of debris moving off my chest as I handed her corpse to my colleague. My heart beats began calming little by little. Then I knew that my hand was the source of the pulse, and not the girl's dead body.

It was the first time to hold a body from which life has departed up to the heavens.

The ambulance set out, with the father attached to it. My heart was broken at his sight, and I appealed to God to avenge him.

*From the Days of Siege*

I saw the team heading towards the side of the street where rockets had been fired. We met up with the rest of our team members, who had left us in the morning to put out a fire.

They told us that the strike did not steal any lives, fortunately. They also checked the three other houses, and they all were empty single-story buildings. Out of caution, the team members stood next to the entrance of every building and loudly called: "Anybody here?". When no answer came but the echo, they would move to the next building.

Before comfort perched in my heart at the thought that all the residents have fled, I heard an answer from the fourth house. A handful of men emerged and invited us to rest with them and eat the breakfast they'd prepared over another story about God's kindness in protecting unarmed citizens from the barbaric aircraft. These people were accustomed to death, and no longer feared it. The men ate their breakfast after they replaced their dishes with new ones clear from dust.

Apparently they were brothers who had bought the land then built their houses adjacently to continue being one family. Only a low wall separates the houses from one another.

They got used to eating breakfast together in one house every Friday. And that day, it was the turn of the oldest brother, whose house was at the beginning of that side of the street.

When the warplanes came, carrying what is known as "sea mines," they planted them along the street. The four men were sitting with their wives and children at the breakfast table. They were more than 30, a mixture of women, children, and men. The mines dropped on the first three homes, while the fourth survived. The breakfast table was still intact in the big dining room.

The eldest brother among them said: "For he whose destiny is to live, nothing will kill him. It's our fate and yours to eat this food. Please, come on and join us!".

Oh God! In which world are these people living? They have grown so used to what is going on! Their belief in fate is their support system.

When our car was heading back to the headquarters, the firefighters were telling their heroic story, which ended with: "We saved seven people from a fire and the eighth died."

I said to myself, "Oh God, we saved one and seven died."

What kind of world is this?

Why all this killing? Whom does it benefit?

## Jako

Jako is the boy I hated at first sight, then loved him when I saw his enthusiasm for his work and his eagerness to rescue people. His story was one I wish I did not know.

The story started when I came to work with the rescue team, and he denounced my presence, and even questioned my intentions, and it ended almost a year later, with a death threat.

When we returned to the center that afternoon, after long hours of hard work, every one of us laid down on their bed. I was perhaps the most

*From the Days of Siege*

exhausted, as I was not used to such tiring work. It seemed I was the first one to sleep while they laughed around me, as though they had not been in direct contact with death only a little while before. They talked about the day's incidents, each in their own way. I slept for an hour and woke up. Some of them were asleep while others were silently flipping through their mobile phones. Jako was alone in a distant corner, away from the other beds. He was hitting his mobile with his palm, cursing the person whom he sold it to. I got up and headed to him, trying to be kind, after I'd seen his devotion to his work.

I walked up, wanting to know the problem with his mobile so that I might help him fix it. I have changed mobile phones several times, so I had some mobile-tech experience. But as soon as he noticed me standing there, my eyes directed to his mobile's screen, he was terrified and moved the mobile phone away, looking at me sharply.

I said to myself, maybe he's still upset about yesterday, especially as Abu Zaid spoke to him harshly after his few passing remarks to me.

"If you have a problem, maybe I can solve it," I said. "I have a lot of experience with mobile phones."

Jako looked at me with the same doubtful gaze and sarcastic smile. He said, as if wanting to test me, "I want to send a video, but the phone's not responding".

"Which program are you using? Maybe the file size is too big?"

"Maybe," he said coldly.

"You can zip the file."

He looked at me curiously and asked.

"How?"

"You can compress the file to reduce its size."

He repeated his question: "How?"

"There's a program to compress files." I reached out my hand and said, "Give me your phone and I'll download the program."

I was afraid, then, when he refused to give me his mobile. He gripped it tightly and said, "You teach me the steps and I can download it myself." At the time, I did not pay attention to his sharp rejection nor his fear at handing over his mobile.

After that, I tried more than once to get close to him, especially as he was mostly alone in his distant corner. They told me that the center had been hit twice when Jako was not around. He would be away for hours, and no one would know where he was.

I grew more curious, and kept trying to break through his solitude, to learn what was behind his childish innocent features. Every time I tried harder to approach him, he grew more distant, until a day came when he shouted in my face: "What do you want from me? Who sent you?". I was surprised by his reaction to my request, where I asked him to guide me to nearby homes of people in need.

Then, out of the blue, he shouted in my face: "Who told you that I'm the neighborhood's mayor who's collecting information about their needs?"

*From the Days of Siege*

"I did not say that, but I asked since you've been in this area longer than I have." And I left him and walked away.

Only a few days later, the center was targeted again. It was hit at the same time Jako disappeared. He left the place half an hour before and never came back.

I did not hear anything from him until that strange message came to me on WhatsApp from an unknown number.

"You thought you were so smart and you wanted to expose me. We still have unfinished business between us. We are yet to meet."

An image came after the text. The photo showed a young guy in military uniform, showing off his muscles and weapon.

In the beginning, I did not recognize him, but when I magnified the photo, I could read on his military uniform the words "The Republican Guard." When I gazed at the young man's aggressive facial features, the innocent childish features of Jako floated to the surface of the photo.

It was Jako! So he went back to the regime that had sent him.

## Lilan Waits for His Mother

Lilan was one of thousands of children who sat behind doors. Behind life's doors, waiting for the return of those who left.

I met him in Aleppo, during the days of siege, in one of the rounds I made trying to meet people and learn about their concerns, sufferings, and needs.

*From the Days of Siege*

There, behind the rubble in an old alley my guide and I barely managed to pass on our way to an ancient "Arab"-style house, that—like the ones around it—was characterized by high fences and the remains of ornamentals climbing the walls before they withered and their flowers died. At the end of the blocked road, there was an old wooden door waiting for us with its fancy copper door-knocker and intricate engravings, indicating that the owner of the house had been rich and lived in opulence. But that day, the house rested in a swamp of destruction. In the early hours of the morning, the atmosphere was filled with careful silence.

I asked my companion who had guided me to the house: "It seems the neighborhood is abandoned?"

He said, while stepping over a pile of debris from a wall that was almost blocking the alley, "No, but most of the residents have left. These are very ancient houses. They're considered antique, and it's forbidden to demolish or rebuild them, as they belong to the registry of international cultural heritage sites. But they could collapse from the roar of a jet breaking the sound barrier before it bombards the area. Residents feared the houses would collapse on them, so some of them left for other places, some went abroad, and others were buried in the rubble."

I smiled to myself when he mentioned the houses belonging to the register as I saw dozens of roofs dangling in the air, revealing their wooden pillars and the secrets lying behind the walls collapsed into piles of mere destruction.

My guide went on:

*From the Days of Siege*

"This house is inhabited by a man coming from a rich family, but now he's poor and disabled and has no income except the aid he receives. His situation is worse than many families we visited yesterday."

He extended his hand to the brass knocker, which sounded sharply through the alley, followed by a gentle echo of the past.

We knocked once...twice...and before the third knock, we were surprised by a squeak from the rusty hinges. It was as though the one who opened the door was standing directly behind it, waiting for our arrival. At the first glimpse, I did not see anyone—as if the door had opened by itself. But when I looked down, I saw a boy looking at me resentfully. He was standing below our line of vision, with his short small body, craning his neck to see our faces.

When my guide said, "Hello sweetie," he looked at us in disappointment, moving his head right and left, then lifting it. It seems he wanted to say, "No, no I do not want it," and maybe he did not like our faces. I saw that through his small disgusted lips. Without saying a single word, he turned his back on us and went inside, leaving the door open.

When I called to him, "Sweetheart, where are your parents?" he turned towards me in anger and said, "My mom isn't here".

I saw his eyes full of two painful tears, which dropped onto his soft cheeks. I felt my heart drop to my feet at this sight.

The sound of a man's voice came from inside, husky and weak: "Boy! Who's at the door?". The child did not answer. It was then that my guide cleared his throat to speak and let the man know we were there, "Oh God".

*From the Days of Siege*

The voice replied from inside, "Come on in! You're welcome! Be careful of the roof over the salon, as it might collapse."

We looked up and saw the sky hovering above us. There was a wide opening from which wooden sticks and the previous roof dangled,. There were clumps of dirt with stones, iron wires, and pieces of cement protruding from every corner. I realized that a huge bomb had penetrated the roof of the salon. We passed through the door quickly, the child walking ahead of us.

We went through a small corridor that connected the outer door with a heavenly courtyard and a dried stone fountain at its center. Withered flowerpots were scattered around the lake, as well as pages torn from books; mixed with plant leaves, branches and plastic bags carried by the wind. Dust covered everything.

The husky voice called again. "Come on in! You're most welcome! Do not judge me though," he added, afraid of being thought inhospitable. After we mounted the two steps to the room's threshold where the voice had come from, I saw the disabled man in the corner.

He did not stand to welcome us, as his legs have been only recently amputated, and his injury was not totally healed. My guide told me about him. A fragment of a barrel bomb had dropped on the neighborhood, amputating both of his legs up to the knee.

He was a handsome man, with prominent cheekbones. He wore an old dirty pajama shirt, his wide chest was hairy and partly exposed. I could not tell his height, but the upper part of his body told story of youth and agility rarely seen.

*From the Days of Siege*

"I cannot stand, do not be offended."

His eager words made me sad inside. Physically, it seems that he must have been able to uproot a tree.

*Many are those sentenced to immediate death by war, but some remain entrapped in their suspended judgements..*

At that collapsed house, I knew the victim had been killed by the war, his fate suspended in the hands of war's atrocities.

The war left him destroyed, with no strength or power. He was abandoned by everyone. Some died, and some immigrated, escaping with their lives. They left with his wife, who had been taking carrying him every week to field hospitals to treat his soft-tissue injuries threatened with inflammation.

He told us, while the child listened:

"[My wife] had searched the whole of Aleppo for a medication to help me. Lately, the medicine has not been available. So, she was forced to travel to visit her family in Al-Atarib, near the border with Turkey, where she might find medicine smuggled in. Can you imagine that Aleppo, a city that was providing everything for its people, has changed into a place that needs medicine from a small village? After she left, the city was besieged, and the ways in and out were cut. She has not yet returned. How can she come back when the roads are besieged?"

His voice rose above the husky tone he'd been speaking in as he uttered this final sentence. He was staring at the child crammed into a distant corner, biting the sides of his fingers, completely disregarding our presence. I asked

*From the Days of Siege*

him, "Why do not you go abroad, where you might find the right medicine and treatment?"

He looked flummoxed: "We immigrated! Who told you we did not? Three months after I was injured, we went with people escaping bombardment into the northern countryside. They carried me on a chair, and we had some money saved a long time ago. I could not bear it. Exile is hard, and to be one of the needy is harder. In all my life, I needed no one but God. I worked in business, and God showered us in goodness but now everything has come to an end. No one is buying and selling, and all my properties are no longer worth a penny. As for this child, I have enrolled him at the best nurseries in the area. He is an outstanding and a hardworking boy. Soon, I found myself disabled, lonely, and displaced in other people's homes. May God reward them all with goodness, as they were quite welcoming. I could not bear it. I preferred death in my home than to be a burden on any other human being. I immigrated, but I could not forget the house I was born in. My father, mother, grandfather, and his grandfather all died here. My soul is attached to this place".

"But you are alone now," I said. "Who will help provide for your needs?"

He waved off the smell of humiliated oppression. "God does not forget anyone, and there are many good people. Believe me, I have never gone to sleep hungry." He gestured to the side of his bed, where I noticed a bag that included pieces of broken bread, as well as another filled with medicine.

"Do not believe that God could forget anyone! I have a neighbor who is one of my childhood friends. He will never abandon me, at least this I am sure

*From the Days of Siege*

of. God reward him with every goodness! He is doing everything in his capacity to cater to my needs. He even carries me to the bathroom."

The man's eyes filled with tears, words choking midway up his throat. A long silence ensued, punctuated by heavy breaths. The only sound came from the child who I was watching us all the time as we sat there, still biting his fingers. He sometimes made strange movements that scared me, especially when he wept. I thought he might be autistic. He seemed to be waiting for his father's silence to explode again: "When will my Mama come?".

I was surprised when his dad screamed at him intensely: "I told you thousands of times, when the route opens. The route is blocked now." The child turned towards us, as if he was doubting his father's words, and asked, "Is it true the route is blocked? Why?".

"Because of the war" the father said with a sharp tone. But the child asked, "Why is there a war? Why did they make a war and block the route? Is it just to keep Mama from coming? I want Mama".

I felt my heart break under the blows of the child's powerful innocent questions that mixed with his tears. Several times, I called him to come near me, but he refused to even look at me. His father said, "I swear, if I could get to you, I'd make you stop talking".

"No mate," I said. "Let the child speak".

"Oh, Mister, but he's difficult. He's made me hate children. I wish I did not have a child. All my calamities are on one side, and he's on the other. I do not know what to tell him. Night and day he nags for his mom, but his mom went to bring me medicine and the route was blocked, so what do I do? We cannot get out of Aleppo, and she cannot come back to us, so what can I do?

From that day, he's stayed here in solitude, not moving from the door. He even refuses to play with the neighbors' children. He does not eat unless I force him to. I swear I do not know what to do with him. God is generous, for He is the best disposer of affairs."

I called the boy again, and, when he refused to come, I got up and went up to him, but his body shrank and moved far away until he attached himself to the wall in the corner.

I asked, whispering, "What's your name?". He did not answer, so I asked again, "Don't you know your name?"

"I know my name," he said sharply. "But I do not want to say it"/

I tried winning him over, "I know your name, it's Muhammed. No, Ahmad. Yes, you're definitely Abdallah. Right?"

He replied with a faint smile, as if mocking my lack of information.

"No. Abdallah's the neighbor's boy. He's my friend." He went on: "You do not know my name!"

"That means your name isn't nice."

"No, it's nice."

"OK, then. What's your name?"

"My name is Lilan."

"Ohhh, Lilan's such a lovely name."

*From the Days of Siege*

I felt happy that the child has started to respond and engage with me, after I had thought he was autistic, since he has been ignoring everything around him.

I reached my hand toward my bag to get his attention as he looked at me curiously. "Do you know what I have inside my bag?" I asked him.

"What?"

I got out papers, and a pen, and pictures of me from camps and schools I have visited.

"These are nice kids. They're my friends."

When I saw his gaze following my hands, I showed him my photos with the children eating and playing in the camps. With every picture, I asked: "Where am I here?"

He would put his small finger on my figure, and then he would ask: "Who's this?"

"My friend," I said.

"Who's she?"

"She's my friend. I have many nice friends. Would you like to be my friend?"

He looked at me, shifting his gaze between me and the pictures, and then said: "But I want something to prove that we're friends".

I was surprised that a child this age would enforce such a condition on me.

*From the Days of Siege*

"You have to go with me and bring me Mama," he said.

"We'll bring her."

"Really?" he said, dubious of the promise I just made.

I nodded my head several times and asked him, before he asked me to promise him further, "Do you know how to draw?". I put a white paper in front of him and started drawing similar to an orange. He stared at me until I connected the lines, and I asked him, "Is it good?".

He did not answer, but looked toward the wide opposite wall, where there was a window crossed with elegant ornamental iron bars. On the window sill, there was a green school bag.

"Is it your bag?" I asked. He nodded, and his eyes said *yes*.

"Bring it, and let's see who draws better."

I felt joy fill me when he agreed and got up, shambling over to bring the bag, much to his father's surprise. He opened the bag and got out a notebook, then turned over drawings. After every page he turned, he looked up at my eyes, as though asking me, "Is it good?".

I whistled to express my surprise at its beauty and show how much I liked it.

He then turned another page and looked carefully at his father. I saw lines that formed a female's head, and he said to me, "This is mama".

He turned several other pages, all carrying the same shape, but in different aspects, so I whispered to him, "Do you want me to draw her for you?".

*From the Days of Siege*

"Really?"

"Do you have colors?"

He stood up and looked hurriedly around the room, scanning every corner. Then he walked out. "I'll bring the colors."

The father, who was watching us carefully, looked at me. He had a gentle smile on his lips. He whispered: "May God reward you with every goodness. It seems the child likes you. He's been refusing to talk for the last two weeks, and he's given me a really hard time, I swear. All his friends in the neighborhood came to him, but he refused to go out and play with them".

"We must find a way to bring him his mother," I said. "I will try to help you, God willing".

He gazed at me deeply and said nothing, but I heard the words stuck in his throat.

The boy brought colors from the other room. We drew many faces but he did not like any, "Mama is more beautiful."

Then he took the pen from my hand and drew a circle for the face and started drawing long line of hair, "Her hair is much longer."

Then we drew fruits. He drew a pair of every type of fruit he knew, "This is for me, and this is for Mama when she comes back".

At the same time, my guide was recording the provisions the home needed, so that we could buy them. I said to Lilan, "What do you think about going to the market to buy some fruits?". Before he could refuse, I added, "If Mama comes back, she should find some for her, right?". Upon hearing my proposition, the boy jumped with happiness. I took his little hand, and we went out together. I had a will to do the impossible, to find a way to reunite him with his mother, and I told him about that.

He bought all kinds of chips, and got two bags of every type and said, "This is for me, and the other is for Mama".

I told him to take whatever he wanted. He wanted to grab something that was up high, and he asked the shopkeeper to help him. "I want some of that."

The shopkeeper said, smiling, "These are hair clips for girls, and you're a boy."

"I know," he said stubbornly.

"Okay then, why? You're a man. What are you going to do with them?"

"This is for my Mama."

He was so happy when we were on our way back. I was happier than him, especially when he saw some of his friends playing in the shadow of a wall and he let go of my hand and ran towards them calling, "Abdallah, Abdallah! Mama will come back. Uncle will bring her back."

The children shouted happily: "Yay! Come on play with us!"

He turned towards me and asked: "Should I play with them?"

"Sure. You should always play with them."

I left him playing with the friends he'd abandoned, according to his father's story.

*Oh God, help me to be faithful to this child and complete his joy,* I said to myself.

When the father saw the bags of chips, he thanked me and said: "Why did you do that, brother? God's graces are many, and He does not leave us in need of anything." This surprised me, as I knew the only food existent in his house was some cracked, dry bread. I remembered a woman in one of the villages in Latakia's countryside. She also showed admirable virtue when we were distributing sums from a charitable man to martyrs' wives. When I gave her the sum allotted her, she took half of it and gave back the other half. When I said, "It's for you," she said, "No, this is enough for me". When I insisted on her, she said: "Oh brother! Yesterday, my husband visited me in a dream and asked me to take only half, as some others need the rest". I was surprised to hear it, but what really amazed me was that when we moved to another area, an old woman came to me asking me to give her the sum, which she'd seen in her dream.

*Whatever happens in war might be unbelievable, but it happens.*

The voice of the disabled man awakened me from my memories.

"The best gift you offered me was to see my son happy again."

"God willing," I said enthusiastically, "I will keep doing it, and I'll find a way to bring back his mother. Do not worry! Give me the address and details, and I'll try to communicate with people who can bring her in." But he kept silent, so I had my doubts growing again.

"Tell me her full name and address," I said.

He did not answer.

*From the Days of Siege*

I felt he did not believe in me, so I pushed on with my offer. "I'll contact friends who have strong connections. You just give me the name and address."

He moved his eyes, which were full of tears, and said in low voice: "The address is: Al-Atarib Cemetery."

I could not understand, but he went on.

"I'm grateful to you, my brother. I swear I know that you would do whatever you could to help, but Lilan's mother died here. She was martyred after a barrel bomb dropped on the public market".

I felt so ashamed of myself for having talked so much and asked to help while he was thinking how to break the news to me. He also said: "We haven't told the child yet. He's still too young to acknowledge such pain".

After a while, I told him that I wished him peace of mind. We asked to leave, and my guide was the first one out, so that Lilan did not see me or the tears filling my eyes while we were walking out of the place.

You have to forgive me Lilan! At this point, I cannot help you. No one can reach someone who is dead. I have also lost many of the people I love.

*When a child loses one of his parents, the hardest question to circulate in your mind, with every hour and every minute, will be "Where is my mom?" .. Can anyone answer that?*

How can this father tolerate the child asking again and again about his mom? Why does not he tell him? What if the child had found out from the owner of the shop we went to? What would happen?

*From the Days of Siege*

We should not hide truth from children and allow hope to grow room within their fragile hearts. They have the right to know and to feel sad for those they love.

\* \* \*

I wrote in my notebook:

Aleppo was neither the first nor the last place to be besieged and destroyed, forcing its people to be displaced. Other Syrian cities—Homs, Madaya, al-Zabadani and many others—faced the same fate. Eastern Ghouta lived under the most horrible types of siege, as half a million humans were besieged for six consecutive years. It ended in the forcible displacement of those who were not killed.

The tragedies of besiegement are more than can be counted. Details of tragedies are deeper than what can be observed man's naked eye. I wrote some of what I lived, and it's less than a fraction. I documented some of what the people of al-Ghouta lived during the siege, retrieving my information from two messages delivered to the world by a doctor and mother.

The mother, Niven, was trying to protect her two children in her arms from bombardment.

She wrote:

"When the bombardment intensifies, I feel my physical structure is incomplete. My two arms are not enough to hug my son and protect him from danger. I cannot bear the idea of my inability to fully cover Qusay and Maya with my arms."

*From the Days of Siege*

Dr. Hussam was close to the victims of the bombardment in the field hospitals. I will include the message he wrote to the world as is. It is the perfect summary of my book:

"My message today is not for world leaders nor for human rights organizations.

My message is for our fellow humans living on this planet.

My message is for everyone who holds their children at night before they fall asleep.

My message is for every mother who bids farewell to her children with lovely kisses before they head off to school.

For every mother, every child, every father and every human, and all of what humanity deeply means:

Listen to me!

This is the twenty-first century, where the world can manage to protect pandas from extinction, and scientists can look into the possibility of life on the other planets in our galaxy.

It is exactly 2018, when the biggest Christmas tree was lit, and the world is still celebrating Nobel Prizes for Peace.

It is the second millennium, according to the Gregorian calendar of that follows Jesus Christ's birth, whose teaching filled the world and spread peace throughout. However, today it is the fifth of the 'Bloody Calendar' documenting the campaign of annihilation against half a million civilians, including children and women, in a spot called Damascus's Ghouta, which

*From the Days of Siege*

disappeared from the satellite screens in our solar system that failed to see the fire and shelling swallowing our children and women.

In our Damascene Ghouta neighborhood, blood seems to hinder the work of those satellites. This is why my colleagues and I decided to send our voices to other galaxies, after living through five hellish sleepless nights of torturous guilt. We hope to find other places in a different galaxy where no barrel bombs and no rockets tear Ghouta's children. Where no jets drop their payload on the heads of women, children and elderly every minute.

This place is one of the few remaining rescue points for the injured who were torn apart, their limbs lost, their eyes cut out. The lives of their babies were stolen, only because they were born on this earth and their blood was not seen by the sensors of artificial satellites and cameras. Hence, they were annihilated in total silence.

Along with some of my colleagues, I got out of the center. Time has become different for us, as we were no longer able to distinguish night from day. The only thing that makes us recognize time is the massacres and body parts carried by rescuers. Their screams tell us that they were standing in queues to get food, and then the death barrels transformed them into torn remains.

We decided to leave the operating rooms, to breathe blood-free air, and to hear—even for a second—the voices of children and women that were not weeping.

So, let us leave!

*From the Days of Siege*

Corridors, waiting rooms, emergency rooms, management offices, and parking lots are all full of hundreds of families that came with their children, from under the rubble of their homes. And they could not go back. They have no place to go to.

The mother put her son on the ground, where we operated on him two days before, as the rooms and beds are fully occupied. His hands shook from the cold, and his mother wept over his head without knowing what to do.

Corpses are scattered between the people sitting in hallways and children crying for their fathers. Women in turn cry for their dead children, and for the impossibility of burying them. Even the cemetery has been targeted, and the mortuary was destroyed.

I saw a child we lost yesterday, after we failed to save his life. His mother lay down beside him on the ground sleeping after she had cried all night for him, surrendering to a deep slumber as she holds him against her torn, blood-covered clothes.

My steps and heartbeat accelerated as I moved between the injured, martyred, and those lying on the ground. I saw a relative of mine sleeping alone in a corner. I ran towards him with hurried steps, but one of his brothers stopped me and said that their sibling died while bringing a loaf of barley bread for his children.

Oh God! What a crime!

He died two days ago while I was treating the wounds of the injured, completely oblivious of his situation. Nobody was able to bury him.

*From the Days of Siege*

When I looked into the ambulance mirror, I did not see tears in my eyes, as I once had, when I bid farewell to child after child. I knew tears have an end, just as the oppressor has an end too.

I decided to go back to the smell of blood. It is more merciful than the atrocities in the corridors and hallways, but an old woman stopped me and said:

"This is my son, who was killed by a blind barrel bomb, and these little children are his. They are all crying around him, do you know why?"

I did not answer. Her eyes filled with tears. "I swear they haven't eaten a bite of food in two days. It's hunger that forced them to cry, these poor orphans."

Oppressors

The world's incapacity to act

The death of humanity

What words can further describe this atrocity I am beholding?

How can the money in my pocket help this lady when all the markets and warehouses are destroyed. There is no food any more in Ghouta, which was once full of life and different fruits. Its alleys are only filled with blood's color and death's smell. No other signs of life.

I sat beside that sixty-year-old grandmother, knowing that nothing can soothe her aching soul, but it was I who felt desperate and powerless. She patted me on the shoulder and said, "If you can bury my son, bury me alive beside him. Since you were unable to save his life, I will be unable to feed his children."

What kind of desperation are we living in the middle of the 21st century? Has humanity lost its essence forever?

What kind of powerlessness is this?

My message today is not for world leaders, kings, security councils or human rights organizations.

My message today is for our fellow humans on this earth.

My message is for those who believe in God's spirit living in their souls.

Listen to me!

Here in Ghouta, there are humans like you. All they wanted was to live decently, nothing more. But they were answered with barrels filled with gunpowder that dropped on their children, and skies was filled with jets throwing bombs on women's heads, and grounds set on fire beneath their feet.

You are our partners on this planet. All we want from you is to prove to your children that you did not leave their innocent counterparts to die, since you are humans yourself, brimming with God's spirit in your hearts.

Tell these angels that you did something to save them and to stop the massacres slaughtering them.

Tell the people that the earth is wide enough for them and their fellow children.

*From the Days of Siege*

If you ignore these massacres and people's blood staining our soil, you have to know that this planet will not bear your existence. As the earth rotates, these massacres will circulate in your brains so deeply that you will never taste the blessing of sleep. You will be deprived from the happiness and pleasure of kissing your children every day. We are sure that God—who did not leave your children hungry or cold—will not abandon us, but the blood of the children of Ghouta is a shame forever clinging to your spines if you dare close your eyes and escape in deliberate ignorance.

Help us save your humanity".

# Unfinished Story

Inside one refugee camp in Turkey's Reyhanli city, I saw a woman sitting apart from the crowds of people. Her gaze drifted toward the south as she moved her head to the right, and then left, peering around the branches of bushes were blocking her vision. She seemed to be staring at an unclear thing standing far away.

I tried to see what she was looking at. I walked up to her bowed back turned to me. Nothing was in front of her except the border fence, behind which was Syrian land. When she sensed my approach, she turned towards me. Wrinkles covered her face, which was wet from the tears that filled her eyes.

"What are you looking for, auntie? Have you lost something?"

She beat her white eyelashes to *indicate yes*.

"What have you lost? Can I help you?"

She smiled amidst her tears and moved her head away, as if telling me it was impossible. She said in a low voice, "I lost my life and soul".

Again, she moved her head and arched back, stretching her neck so she could look forward. Then she took a deep breath, as though she wanted to swallow the cold breeze that was coming from the south.

"Please, tell me, what are you looking for?"

*Unfinished Story*

"I'm searching for their smell. I'm trying to see their graves back there in Homs, where I left them. There were thirteen of them, and I left them in one grave, covered by the roof of the house."

She extended a finger, pointing toward the south while sniffling, and said, "Look with me! Do you see them there?"

Along her line of sight, more than 300 kilometers separated us from Homs.

"Do not be afraid, I can see them."

She struck her chest with her fist and said, "They're here."

She drove her fingers into her eyes and said, "They are here."

She stood up and headed towards the border, leaving me confused and unable to reply.

I left her, as I felt she wanted to be alone. I said to myself that I would express solidarity with her the next time, when she would feel a tad better.

I looked at her bowed back, as she leaned against her cane, and her shaking steps. I did not see a woman. I saw a mountain moving with a cane. Even the mountain would not be able to carry what she was carrying.

When I looked for her the next day, I could neither find her, nor could I learn any news of her. She disappeared with her story before I could write it in my notebook, leaving empty lines amidst million other stories that died and disappeared when their bearers vanished.

# Last Call for Peace

This is but the tip of the iceberg of the stories I have lived through up until this point in my mortal life.. Even though it will not be repeated, the desire to leave this world occupied me for quite a while, after I realized how cruel the human race is. I never dreamt of being a father so that my son would not end up becoming an orphan, or that I would not live this life as a childless father. I dream of carrying with me all the angels of the earth who have paid the heavy price of adults' sins.

After all I have lived and suffered, after all the still ongoing pains of war that I have seen. After all I have read about other wars that took place in history, which we heard from real fighters, widows or orphans left behind by the war. After all the martyrs have departed for their heavens, leaving those crawling in the big black pit. After all the tragedies of war I saw in my country, I wrote in my notebook:

No to wars.

No to wars.

No to wars with anybody or for any reason. War is a human-run mill that grinds their souls, no matter which fighting party they belong to. In between the grinding rocks, thousands of innocent lives are crushed, while leaders of every belligerent party raise the flag of heroism, and medals of victory; believing their names are the ones written eternally on the walls of history. In fact, they have been forever engraved on people's skulls. How many victims have been sacrificed by invaders to present their leaders with gold-

*Last Call for Peace*

plated victory? How many victims have been killed so that colonizing nations can build their empires?

Humans of both sides, be them colonizers or the colonized, are all victims.

You who wage these wars, is it not time for you to make peace?

War is a mill for human lives that reveal the worst face of human behavior.

It endangers not only the continuity of the human race, but also the earth in its entirety. God sent humans to earth to build it, not destroy it and shed the blood of their fellow brothers and sisters. This earth is but a mere speck in this vast universe, and it is but an absurd reality to wage ferocious wars on a fleeting particle in space.

Perhaps Carl Sagan, the renowned astrophysicist, summarized this better when he wrote about the earth in his book 1994 *Pale Blue Dot*:

From this distant vantage point, the Earth might not seem of any particular interest.

but for us, it's different.

"Look again at that dot. That's here. That's home. That's us. On it everyone you love, everyone you know, everyone you ever heard of, every human being who ever was, lived out their lives. The aggregate of our joy and suffering, thousands of confident religions, ideologies, and economic doctrines, every hunter and forager, every hero and coward, every creator and destroyer of civilization, every king and peasant, every young couple in love, every mother and father, hopeful child, inventor and explorer, every teacher of morals, every corrupt politician, every "superstar," every "supreme leader," every saint and sinner in the history of our species lived there -- on a mote of dust suspended in a sunbeam.

The Earth is a very small stage in a vast cosmic arena. Think of the rivers of blood spilled by all those generals and emperors so that, in glory and triumph, they could become the momentary masters of a fraction of a dot. Think of the endless cruelties visited by the inhabitants of one corner of this pixel on the scarcely distinguishable inhabitants of some other corner, how frequent their misunderstandings, how eager they are to kill one another, how fervent their hatreds.

Our posturings, our imagined self-importance, the delusion that we have some privileged position in the Universe, are challenged by this point of pale light. Our planet is a lonely speck in the great enveloping cosmic dark. In our obscurity, in all this vastness, there is no hint that help will come from elsewhere to save us from ourselves.

The Earth is the only world known so far to harbor life. There is nowhere else, at least in the near future, to which our species could migrate. Visit, yes. Settle, not yet. Like it or not, for the moment the Earth is where we make our stand.

It has been said that astronomy is a humbling and character-building experience. There is perhaps no better demonstration of the folly of human conceits than this distant image of our tiny world. To me, it underscores our responsibility to deal more kindly with one another, and to preserve and cherish the pale blue dot, the only home we've ever known."

*Last Call for Peace*

While we sit on this 'pale blue dot' witnessing the burning of our homeland, we still stare at the distant horizon searching for the light of peace, goodness and safety for us and for all humanity. We do suffer from heartbreak indeed, but no doubt that those who are humane feel our pain.

Our salvation is a comfort for us and for every awakened conscience.

In the dark era we live in where the conscience of humanity makes careless, hateful stances out like a dragon emitting its grudge over humanity's paths that lead to prosperity and happiness.

Amid this conflict, I ask myself, how can I live happily while others are getting tortured by endless pain?

These wars, tragedies and injustices are not committed by the inhabitants of another planet but by brutal leaders whose presence overshadows like monsters who have wreaked havoc in this world. I dream that one day, these monsters revert to their human nature and stop shedding rivers of blood. I hope humans work together and unite to stop this bloodshed, alleviate the suffering of the world and release the remaining hope from under the rubble.

Some humanitarian organizations have tried and relatively succeeded in healing some of the wounds and relieving some of humanity's pains regurgitating lava of pain and suffering.

What is happening in Syria is horrible beyond imagination. Somehow it seems a mere delusion, a figment of man's imagination. False media and biased news agencies have long been warping the state of reality as it is on Syrian soil. Those who have invested great efforts to obscure the experiences of these innocent lives and obstruct the justice that should and will undoubtedly, sooner or later, reign. However, thanks to the tele-communication revolution we are experiencing, at least some of the truth has been documented.

Yet, what has been hidden and disappeared under the war's rubble is far greater and more terrifying.

Dear readers, for those of you who think you have no power to change these unjust events, rest assured that you are playing your part already by baring witness to a segment of the truth.

Through your pure beings and your dedicated time to inquire about our journey, at least the essence of this authentic story will be carried and shall continue to live and survive. Perhaps through continuing to spread the real word of these Syrian ordeals you can further your part in the story, so that we can at least increase the momentum that is needed in establishing international solidarity and understanding.

Printed in Great Britain
by Amazon